Primary Sources of World Cultures ™

ENGLAND

A PRIMARY SOURCE CULTURAL GUIDE

Graham Faiella

The Rosen Publishing Group's
PowerPlus Books™
New York

Published in 2005 by The Rosen Publishing Group, Inc.
29 East 21st Street, New York, NY 10010

Library of Congress Cataloging-in-Publication Data

Faiella, Graham.
England: a primary source cultural guide/by Graham Faiella.
    p. cm.—(Primary sources of world cultures)
Summary: An overview of the history and culture of England and its people including the geography, myths, arts, daily life, education, religion, and government, with illustrations from primary source documents. Includes bibliographical references and index.
ISBN 1-4042-2911-6 (library binding)
1. England—Juvenile literature. [1. England.]
I. Title. II. Series.
DA27.5.F35 2004
942—dc22

                                                                                2003022032

Manufactured in the United States of America

Cover Images: Background: 1225 version of the Magna Carta; at left: Windsor Castle, London; at right: A bobby, or London policeman.

CONTENTS

Introduction .7

1 **The Land**
The Geography and Environment
of England .11

2 **The People**
From the Stone Age to the
Space Age .23

3 **The Languages of England**
From Old English to
Modern English 33

4 **English Myths and Legends** 43

5 **English Festivals and Ceremonies
of Antiquity and Today** 53

6 **The Religions of England
Throughout History** 61

7 **The Art and Architecture
of England** 71

8 **The Literature and
Music of England** 79

9 **Famous Foods and Recipes**
   of England 87

10 **Daily Life and Customs**
   in England 95

11 **Education and Work**
   in England 105

England at a Glance 112

   History 112
   Economy 113
   Government and Politics 114
   Timeline 116
   Map .118
   Fact Sheets 119

Glossary 122

For More Information 123

For Further Reading 124

Bibliography 124

Primary Source Image List 125

Index .127

INTRODUCTION

England is one of three countries that make up Great Britain. The other two countries are Scotland (to the north) and Wales (to the west). These three countries, plus Northern Ireland, make up the United Kingdom (UK). The term "Britain" is often used to refer to the United Kingdom as a whole. People from Britain are British subjects (citizens). They come from England, Scotland, Wales, or Northern Ireland. It is a big mistake to use the term "English" for someone from Wales, Scotland, or Northern Ireland. An English person comes from England, just as a Welsh person comes from Wales, a Scot from Scotland, and a Northern Irishman from Northern Ireland. A British person is therefore anyone who comes from the United Kingdom of Great Britain and Northern Ireland, which is the official name for the UK.

The British Isles include Great Britain (England, Scotland, and Wales), the whole

Pictured opposite is part of Hadrian's Wall, which was built by the Romans in AD 122. Hadrian's Wall stretches 75 miles (120 km) across Great Britain. The wall separated Roman-conquered Britain from the invading Scottish tribes in the north. Pictured above is Coniston Water, a lake in Cumbria, England. Coniston Water is the third-largest lake in England's Lake District.

This is a view showing the Houses of Parliament and the Clock Tower. The Clock Tower is the home of Big Ben, a world-famous, 13.8-ton bell. Besides Big Ben, there are also four smaller bells that play the Westminster chimes every fifteen minutes.

island of Ireland (Northern Ireland and the separate, independent Republic of Ireland in the south), the Channel Islands and Isle of Man (both of which have a certain amount of self-governance), and all the various other English, Welsh, Scottish, and Irish islands dotted around the coast.

For the past 1,500 years the English way of life has evolved in relative isolation. In part that is because England is part of an island nation—the United Kingdom—separated by the sea from continental Europe. The last time England was invaded by a foreign power was in 1066, by the French Norman duke William the Conqueror. The character of "Englishness" has remained remarkably consistent over the centuries. England today, however, is becoming a culturally

Dorset, England, has many bluebell woods such as this one in Kingcombe. Bluebell woods are forests that are carpeted by bluebells in the springtime. Bluebells are a type of hyacinth with periwinkle bell-shaped, fragrant flowers.

This nineteenth-century illustration by Thomas Allom depicts the Port of London. The Port of London lies along the banks of the river Thames. During the eighteenth and nineteenth centuries, it was the busiest port in the world.

diverse society. Immigrants from former British Empire countries started to arrive in the mid-twentieth century. The United Kingdom joined the European Union in 1973. England is now an equal partner in European affairs. American and other cultural influences are changing the English lifestyle. The Spanish philosopher George Santayana (1863–1952) wrote in 1922 that "England is the paradise of individuality . . ." He meant that the English are proud of their independent spirit. They are still proud of their "individuality." Their "Englishness," however, is changing faster than ever before in their history.

A field in Zennor, Cornwall, is blanketed with purple heather and yellow gorse. Cornwall is known for its scenic countryside. Natural attractions such as Land's End, Bodmin Moor, and the Lost Gardens of Heligan draw many visitors every year to Cornwall.

THE LAND

The Geography and Environment of England

England is surrounded by water (except along its northern boundary with Scotland and part of its western border with Wales). The Irish Sea and the Atlantic Ocean lie to the west. The English Channel is to the south, separating the UK from France and the rest of Europe. The North Sea lies to the east. No place in England is more than about 100 miles (161 kilometers) away from the coast. The land area of England is 50,516 square miles (130,834 sq km). This makes it the largest country in the United Kingdom, which has a total land area of 94,161 square miles (243,876 sq km).

Although England is still a "green and pleasant land," as the poet William Blake (1757–1827) wrote in his poem-hymn "Jerusalem," it is primarily an industrial country. People live in mainly high-density groups of towns and cities. Only a few parts of England have been untouched by human occupation. The Countryside Agency has classified thirty-seven places in England and Wales as Areas of Outstanding Natural Beauty (AONB) in its efforts to protect the countryside from urban growth.

Pictured at left are the white cliffs of Dover in Kent. The cliffs are composed of chalk, a soft white mineral. Chalk's resistance to erosion causes it to form in steep, clifflike formations. Pictured above is a street scene in the town of Broadway in the Cotswolds. The Cotswolds is a hilly region with many peaceful, medieval villages. Many Britons vacation in or retire to the Cotswolds.

A field of oilseed rape flowers (rapeseed) extends across the countryside. English rapeseeds are harvested for animal feed and for vegetable oil that is used in cooking. England's damp, temperate climate creates perfect growing conditions for this plant.

Climate

The warm-water current known as the Gulf Stream is the most important influence on England's climate. England is situated as far north as southern Canada, but its climate is much milder. Westerly winds blow in from the Atlantic. As they pass over the Gulf Stream, they pick up heat and moisture. This warm, humid air keeps England's climate temperate. Winter temperatures rarely dip below freezing, except in the north of England. Summer temperatures average 68° Fahrenheit (20° Celsius) and only occasionally get above 86°F (30°C). The hottest temperature ever recorded in England was just over 100°F (38°C) in August 2003.

Snow covers the higher hills and mountains of northern England for about fifty days per year. In the south, snow is rare. England has a reputation as having a wet climate. However, England's average rainfall of 35 to 40 inches per year (89 to 102 centimeters per year) is less than that of Houston, Miami, or New Orleans. It is about the same as the average rainfall for Washington, D.C.

This is a view of the rocky coast of Land's End. Land's End is a peninsula located in Cornwall. It is the westernmost tip of England.

The Southwest and West Country

The Isles of Scilly lie 25 miles (40 km) to the southwest of Land's End, the most southwestern point of mainland England. These small islands have a population of less than 2,500. On the mainland itself, the southwestern counties of Devon and Cornwall are some of the most popular places in England for summer vacations. This part of England has rolling hills, steep valleys, a mild climate, and a coastline of many small bays, harbors, and sandy beaches. Dartmoor National Park in Devon is England's last real wilderness and biggest open space. Dairy farms around this part of England are particularly numerous. Tin was mined in Cornwall for thousands of years, but that has now stopped.

Farther north is the rolling countryside of Gloucestershire (pronounced GLOS-ter-sher) and the Cotswold Hills. Small villages built from the honey-colored local limestone are characteristic of the Cotswolds. On the edge of the Cotswolds is the city of Oxford. Oxford University, founded in the twelfth century, is one of the world's greatest centers of higher education.

The South and Southeast

London is the focal point of the south of England and is the capital city of the United Kingdom. The counties of Surrey, Hampshire, Sussex, and East Sussex to the south of London are among the wealthiest counties of England. Kent is known as the Garden County because it used to produce so many food crops, especially for the London markets. All around London are small towns, busy roads, and railways, and seacoast tourist towns that still attract millions of visitors every year. Many of the towns around the south of England look quite new. This is because German bombing during World War II (1939–1945) destroyed many buildings, which had to be rebuilt after the war.

Along the coast, towns such as Brighton, Margate, and Ramsgate became popular in the late 1800s as seaside resorts. Dover, on the south coast, is England's main gateway port to France, just 22 miles (35 km) across the English Channel. Along this part of the south coast, the white cliffs of Dover are prominent. These high cliffs, made of soft chalk, have become a symbol of England. They are the first view of England that most people see when they cross the English Channel by ferry from the Continent.

The area to the north and northeast of London stretches away to low hills and the flat, open spaces of East Anglia. The University of Cambridge, in the town of that name, was founded in 1209. Cambridge and its traditional rival, Oxford, are England's most prestigious universities. In the county of Norfolk, the Broads is a system of marshy inland waterways that is an important wildlife sanctuary. Between the cities of Lincoln and Cambridge are the fens. This 15,500-square-mile (40,145 sq km) area of reclaimed flooded marshlands is among the richest farmland in all of southern England.

The river Thames flows from the Cotswold Hills, through London, and out to the North Sea at the Thames Estuary. At 205 miles (330 km), it is the longest river in England. The river is tidal downstream from Teddington, just west of London, rising and falling up to 22 feet (7 meters) with the tide. In 1982, a barrier was completed across the Thames near Woolwich, east of London, to control flooding. Until the 1960s, the Thames was a busy commercial waterway. Barges, colliers, and seagoing ships all used the Thames to carry cargo and passengers to and from London. Today, the river is mostly used by sightseeing boats and small passenger craft.

The Midlands: Heart of England

The Midlands stretches from the North Sea coast in the east to the border with Wales on the west. The Midlands is best known for its industries: the potteries (china and ceramics) around Stoke-on-Trent in Staffordshire; automobiles around Coventry and Birmingham; shoes around Northampton; and railway manufacturing at Derby. Many

Coniston Water is located in the Lake District. This lake is dominated by the mountain called Coniston Old Man.

of the polluting industries of this area have now declined. Some parts of the Midlands, such as the Malvern Hills in Worcestershire and the Lincolnshire Wolds, are protected as Areas of Outstanding Natural Beauty.

The North: Industry, Moors, Dales, and Lakes

The northwest was the cradle of the Industrial Revolution in eighteenth- and nineteenth-century England. Coal mining, steel, textiles, and shipbuilding were all concentrated there. Many of those industries have since declined or disappeared altogether. The north of England has areas of great natural beauty sandwiched between the old industrial towns. The Lake District National Park has England's biggest lake, Windermere (6 sq miles; 16 sq km). The Yorkshire Dales and the North York Moors National Parks are rugged and dramatic. The Pennine

A colt and a young mare graze in a pasture near a village in Robin Hood's Bay in North Yorkshire. Robin Hood's Bay is a historic fishing village that was once a popular port for smugglers.

The windswept North York Moors are the largest stretch of heather moorlands in Britain. The North York Moors are a famous landscape featured in *Wuthering Heights* and *Jane Eyre*, two classic British novels.

Hills are austere and bleak. The Peak District is popular for hiking. During the Roman occupation of Britain, the emperor Hadrian (AD 117–138) built a wall 73 miles (117 km) long across the north of England. Known now as Hadrian's Wall, it stretches from just north of the city of Carlisle on the west coast to near the east coast city of Newcastle-upon-Tyne. Its original purpose was to stop the people in the north (meaning, in those days, the Scots) from invading England.

The Great Cities: London, Manchester, Birmingham, and Liverpool

London

London is at least three cities: Greater London, including the center and suburbs; Central London; and the City of London, the "square mile" city founded by the

Romans as a walled settlement and which is today one of the world's most important financial centers. London was founded by the Romans in the first century on the north bank of the Thames. They called it Londinium. Today, it is England's main cultural center, a world financial power, and the seat of government for the whole United Kingdom.

Manchester

The Romans built a fort on the northwest coast called Mamucium, the city we now call Manchester. In the eighteenth and nineteenth centuries, England's cotton textile and clothing industries boomed in Manchester. Greater Manchester grew to a population of more than 2 million. The 37-mile-long (60 km long) Manchester Ship Canal, which opened in 1894, made the city an important port until the 1980s. Today, most of the old textile mills have been converted into other industrial uses. People from Manchester are called Mancunians.

Birmingham

Birmingham dates from the twelfth century. In the eighteenth century, Birmingham was the center of Britain's Industrial Revolution. Today, Birmingham is a center of light engineering and small industries. It is sometimes called the City of 1,001 Trades because of the diversity of its industries. The world's first steam engines were built in Birmingham. The city has 32 miles (51 km) of canals (Venice

A field in West Sussex is used for hay production. Apart from its fields, Sussex also has a range of hills known as South Downs. The tallest hill, Ditchling Beacon is more than 800 feet (244 m) tall.

has only 28 miles [45 km] of canals). Birmingham is colloquially known as Brummagem. People from Birmingham are called Brummies.

Liverpool

Liverpool, on the river Mersey, became a fishing port in the Middle Ages. The first of its 7 miles (11 km) of docks was built in 1715. By 1800, Liverpool was England's largest port. In 1830, the Liverpool and Manchester Railway opened. This was the first railroad in England to link two large cities (the first railroad in England was built in 1825). Liverpool's seagoing trade and its docks declined in the mid-twentieth century. In the 1960s, the rock-and-roll group the Beatles put Liverpool back on the world map.

In June 2003, Liverpool was selected to be the European City of Culture for 2008. Each year a different European Union country has the opportunity to choose its own European City of Culture for that year. The United Kingdom's designated year is 2008. For one year Liverpool will host major cultural events and exhibitions to highlight its cultural heritage as an important European city.

Plants and Animals of England

England used to be covered by woodland forests. Today woodland covers just 7 percent of England's land area. The wood from those old forests (especially oak) was used for building material, such as for ships in the sixteenth and seventeenth centuries. The land was cleared to grow crops and to create space for towns and cities. The wild plants (flora) and animals (fauna) of England now struggle to adapt to live side by side with humans. Commercial farming has reduced the habitat of native flora and fauna. Thousands of miles of hedgerows (thick, high growths of bushes and brambles), a natural habitat for a wide range of plants and animals, have been dug up to create bigger fields for cereal crops, including wheat and barley.

Plants

Trees such as oak, elm, hazel, beech, ash, and yew are found in all corners of England. The oak is the symbol of old-fashioned English values: sturdy, stocky, solid, and strong. The yew is found commonly in cemeteries. It grows to a great age, often

Pictured at left is a thick wood in Cornwall. Many woods such as these have been cut down over the past century. Groups such as the Woodland Trust work to preserve the ancient woods by fund-raising and replanting.

A dwarf oak forest called Wistman's Wood in Dartmoor, Devon. Dwarf oaks are shrublike trees that have a stubby, twisted appearance. They usually form dense and tangled forests.

older than 500 years. Elms were almost wiped out in London in the 1950s by Dutch elm disease. A colorful variety of wildflowers in spring and summer illuminates the edges of country lanes and open fields and meadows. Heathers, from purple to orange to yellowish brown, are common over moors and downs (wild, open lands with few trees). The most common plants in England are grasses, which are cultivated for grazing livestock.

Animals

England is along the migration route for hundreds of species of birds. Some waterbirds, such as puffins, fly out to sea for several months. They then return to nesting sites along the coast. Other water species such as guillemots, shags (cormorants), gannets, and herring gulls nest all along the coast of Britain. The most common small permanent residents inland are sparrows, wrens, tits, jays, and

magpies (the last being notorious for attacking other species). Rooks (crows) have been most successful in adapting from an ancient woodland habitat to today's highly cultivated and densely populated countryside. On the rough upland moorlands of England, grouse are hunted as a seasonal game bird.

The kestrel, a relative of the falcon, is one of the most common raptors in all of Europe. This male kestrel is perched on a tree in Derbyshire.

A dormouse feasts on the blossoms of a fruit tree. The dormouse's diet consists of berries, flowers, nuts, and insects.

Birds of prey such as kestrels, peregrine falcons, and hawks are common throughout England, but they are more numerous in the north.

Only a few mammal species are native to England. These include voles, shrews, bats, hare, roe and red deer, otters, badgers, and stoats. Gray and common seals are often seen along the coasts. The gray squirrel, introduced from North America in the nineteenth century, has become very common, even to the point of being a pest. Rabbits were cultivated in Norman times, a thousand years ago, for their meat and fur. They have since overrun the countryside in large numbers.

The dormouse used to be a common native rodent. It is now on the verge of extinction. The harvest mouse is also in decline. Foxes have adapted to be common scavengers around the suburbs of towns and cities. Hedgehogs in England have a reputation as cute little country-side animals. Badgers also have a big fan club.

A pair of badgers hunts for food at night. Badgers are skilled diggers. They use their sharp claws to dig up roots and insect nests full of delicious larvae. Badgers also eat frogs, fallen fruit, and bird eggs.

THE PEOPLE

From the Stone Age to the Space Age

ngland is about the same size as the combined U.S. states of North Carolina, Alabama, and New York. Its population of 48 million, however, is much bigger than the 30 million of those three states. The population (or demographic) density of England is 950 people per square mile (367 per sq km), compared to 75 people per square mile (30 per sq km) in the United States. England is, in fact, one of the most densely populated countries in the world. About 95 percent of the English population is white Caucasian. Immigrants from the old British Empire—Indians, Pakistanis, and Bangladeshis from the Indian subcontinent, and West Indians from the Caribbean—started arriving in England after World War II to look for jobs. Most immigrants now live in and around large towns and cities. The society of rural England is, however, still almost entirely white Caucasian.

The Earliest Inhabitants:
From Stone Age to Iron Age

From 70,000 to 8,000 BC, glaciers covered England. Sea levels then were much lower than they are today. People could walk from mainland Europe to the British Isles. These Old Stone Age people were hunter-gatherers, which means they hunted

Pictured at left is the mysterious monument of Stonehenge on the Salisbury Plain in Wiltshire, England. Stonehenge is widely believed to have been built between 2500 and 2000 BC. Today it is one of the most visited places in England. Pictured above, a London bobby (policeman) stands watch at Buckingham Palace in London during the changing of the guard.

wild animals and gathered plants to eat. They lived in small groups of a few families in caves or temporary shelters.

Between 8,300 and 3,500 BC, the climate warmed up. The glaciers melted and the sea level rose. By around 3,000 BC, the British Isles had become islands separated from the European mainland. The people living in southern England at the time were Iberians, rather short, dark-haired people originally from the Mediterranean area. They probably mixed with central European people who came to England. On the high ground of southwest England, these two groups settled as the first permanent inhabitants of England. They built the stone circle known as Stonehenge, on Salisbury (SALS-bury) Plain. Why they built Stonehenge and how they moved the 40- to 50-ton (41 to 51 tonnes) stones around are still mysteries.

The Celts

Tribes of people known as Celts (KELTS) moved into southern England from central Europe starting around 700 BC. The tall, fair-haired Celts mixed with the Iberians. The Celts established tribal communities and shared the work of planting crops, plowing, and clearing forests. They laid out fields using boundaries we can sometimes still see today. The first towns in England and the earliest coin money date from this period known as the Iron Age (700–100 BC). A greater variety of metal implements and the introduction of the plow were the main features of the Iron Age in Britain.

Italian artist Vittorio Raineri made this print in the early 1800s. The print depicts ancient Celts preparing for battle. A Celtic general wearing a winged helmet and fur cloak raises his sword before an attack.

This is a thirteenth-century Byzantine mosaic of Constantine the Great. Constantine rebuilt the Hellenic city Byzantium and named it Nova Roma. After his death, the city became the capital of the Roman Empire and was renamed Constantinople (present-day Istanbul).

The Romans

The Roman emperor Julius Caesar (100–44 BC) knew about the Britons in the land that the Romans called Britannia. Caesar and his armies invaded Britannia in 55 and 54 BC but retreated after fighting the Celts. A hundred years later, in AD 43, the emperor Claudius (10 BC–AD 54) invaded again. This time the Romans stayed. Britannia became a province of Rome for 400 years. The Roman occupation was concentrated in the area we know today as England. The Romans built military towns for their soldiers. London (Londinium), in the south, and York, which Romans called Eboracum, in the north, were the sites of their two main garrisons. The hot springs at the old Roman town of Aquae Solis (now called Bath) are still in use today at that town's Roman baths. The Romans also built 5,000 miles (8,047 km) of roads and introduced new crops (oats, rye, turnips, and celery). Emperor Constantine the Great (AD 306–337) introduced Christianity into Britannia in the fourth century AD. When barbarian tribes conquered Rome in AD 410, Roman rule in Britannia ended.

Angles, Saxons, Jutes, and Vikings

Angles, Saxons, Jutes, and Vikings were Germanic invaders from northern European lands that today include Germany and Denmark. These post-Roman invaders settled most of England and became what we recognize today as the first "English" people. The Angles and Saxons (Anglo-Saxons) dominated. There were hundreds of Anglo-Saxon kingdoms, big and small, and more than 200 kings. In 757, Offa was the first ruler to claim that he was "king of the whole land of the English."

MAR E

The Bayeux Tapestry is 230 feet (70 m) long and has fifty-eight scenes that tell the story of the Norman Conquest and the Battle of Hastings. The creator of the tapestry is unknown today, though many believe that it was woven by Queen Matilda of Flanders, the wife of William the Conqueror.

The most important Anglo-Saxon king and one of the greatest kings in England's history was Alfred the Great (849–899). Alfred was a scholar, soldier, administrator, and educator. In 886, Alfred established a peace treaty with the Vikings. They had been raiding England's east coast since 797. Alfred and the Danish (Viking) king Guthrum agreed that the Danes could settle and control the northeast of England. Alfred would control the south and west. Eventually, three Danish kings even ruled all of England for a while: Cnut (Canute, in English; d. 1035), Harold (d. 1040), and Hardecanute (1019–1042).

The Norman Conquest

In 1066, the Saxon king Edward the Confessor (1003–1066) died. Harold, Earl of Wessex, was declared the new king. But William, Duke of Normandy (in France), and Harold Hardrada, king of Norway, also claimed the English throne. The new king Harold defeated the invading army of the Norwegian king in September 1066,

In 1985, the 900th anniversary of William the Conqueror's Domesday Book, a new version was published for students, historians, and enthusiasts.

at the Battle of Stamford Bridge in northern England. A few days later, William, Duke of Normandy, invaded with an army from France, across the English Channel. Harold marched his army south. On a hill near the south coast town of Hastings, Harold and William clashed. Harold was killed. William was crowned King William I (famously known as William the Conqueror) on Christmas Day, 1066. The Norman Conquest introduced feudalism into England. In the feudal system, the king owned all the land. He divided his power among lords, barons, knights, and other nobles. They governed the ordinary people—the serfs (slaves) and peasants—who cultivated the land in the service of their lord and the king.

The Normans were ruthless and tyrannical rulers but also great organizers and administrators. Soon after he became king, William decided to carry out a survey of "this land [England], how it was peopled and with what sort of men." The survey was a complete description of England at the time. It included everything from the number of animals and people in every village to a description of every field and house in the land. All the details were collected and compiled in two volumes called the Domesday Book, completed in 1086. William's kingdom was spread far and wide. The Domesday Book was essential for William to administer and maintain his authority over his realm.

This is the third version of the Magna Carta that was issued in 1225 by Henry II. The original Magna Carta was issued in 1215, but it was reissued several times later to give additional freedoms to the English people.

The Magna Carta

Barons were the link between the king and his subjects. In the reign of King John (1167–1216), the barons rebelled against the king's abuse of royal power. The barons and the king met at a place called Runnymede (near Windsor, just outside London), in 1215. The barons presented John with a petition outlining their rights and privileges. The petition was called the Magna Carta (Great Charter). Its aim was to reestablish the supremacy of common law, which protected the people against excessive royal power. No man—including the king—could be above the law. The Magna Carta led to the establishment of a committee of twenty-four barons to make sure that the king kept to the terms of the charter. The committee was the forerunner of Parliament as an instrument of democratic government. Today, the Magna Carta, just as the U.S. Constitution does, continues to guarantee fair justice for all people in the United Kingdom under a parliamentary democracy.

Henry VIII and the English Church

One of the great conflicts between the English monarchy and the Catholic Church (the dominant church at the time across all Europe) came with the reign of Henry VIII (1491–1547). Most famously, Henry had six wives.

When Henry came to power in 1509, England was Catholic. His first wife, Catherine of Aragon, gave birth to one daughter. But Henry needed a son to inherit his throne and carry on the Tudor name.

Henry then wanted a divorce from Catherine to marry Anne Boleyn (one of Catherine's ladies of honor), in the hope that she

This is a full-length portrait of Henry VIII by Bavarian artist Hans Holbein the Younger. Holbein painted in the northern Renaissance style and was commissioned to do several portraits for Henry VIII and his brides.

might bear him a son. The pope refused to grant Henry a divorce. Henry had his marriage to Catherine declared invalid anyway. He married Anne Boleyn soon after. She did not give birth to an heir and was beheaded in May 1536. Henry finally had a son (Edward VI; 1537–1553) and heir from his third wife, Jane Seymour. Henry hated the control that

The Six Wives of Henry VIII

Catherine of Aragon (1485–1536; married 1509–1533)
Anne Boleyn (circa 1507–1536; married 1533–1536)
Jane Seymour (1509?–1537; married 1536–1537)
Anne of Cleves (1515–1557; married 1540)
Catherine Howard (1521–1542; married 1540–1542)
Catherine Parr (1512–1548; married 1543–1547)

Anne of Cleves

the Catholic pope in Rome had over England. By the Act of Supremacy in 1534, Henry declared himself supreme head of the Church of England. In 1536, Henry started to dissolve all the monasteries in England. The elimination of the pope's influence in England was largely completed by the dissolution of the monasteries. Equally important, their wealth of jewels, church treasures, and huge tracts of land became the king's property. The Church of England and Henry were still Catholic but were no longer controlled by the pope.

Henry VIII had pushed, threatened, twisted arms, and cut off a few heads to get what he wanted. He used Parliament to create the kind of nation-state that England became by the time of his death in 1547. He incorporated Wales into England through acts of Parliament in 1536 and 1543, as a first step toward the future United Kingdom. He built the first warships with side cannons. He founded the Royal Navy. He established an English national church, separate from Rome, with himself (and future British monarchs) as its head.

Henry's reign marked the end of an English feudal society that owed allegiance only to the Crown and the beginning of modern parliamentary democracy in England. As Henry himself said about Parliament in 1543, his own highest royal status was achieved "when we [i.e., Henry] as head and you as members [of Parliament] are conjoined [joined] and knit together in one body politic."

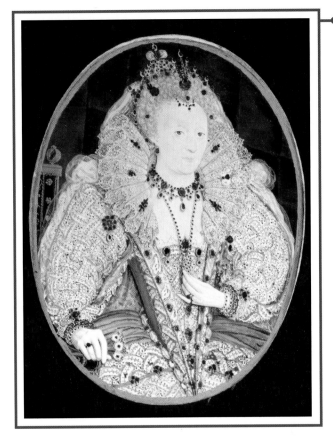

A miniature portrait of Queen Elizabeth I. Queen Elizabeth I is sometimes called the Virgin Queen because she never married and never produced an heir to the throne. On Elizabeth I's death in 1603, the rule of the Tudor dynasty ended in England.

The Elizabethan Age

The Elizabethan age is regarded as a golden age for England. Elizabeth I (1533–1603), the daughter of Henry VIII and Anne Boleyn, ruled by a combination of intelligence, charm, and power. In 1559, the Act of Supremacy made the Church of England the official state church and the queen its supreme governor. England by this time was becoming increasingly Protestant. Phillip II of Spain (1527–1598) was Catholic and fiercely anti-Protestant. In 1588, Phillip sent his navy (the Spanish Armada) to invade England. In the English Channel, the Armada was outgunned by the English navy and wrecked by storms before limping back to Spain. The English defeat of the Armada was a turning point in history. It showed the rest of the world that England was now master of the seas, which led to the origin of the British Empire in the nineteenth century.

The British Empire

Queen Victoria (1819–1901) reigned for sixty-four years, longer than any other British monarch. England and the English people experienced greater changes in the Victorian era than at any time in their history. The British Empire expanded around the world, through trade, commerce, and subjugation. The jewel in the crown of that empire was India. It seems remarkable that a small country such as England could establish control over so many countries around the world for more than a century.

It could do so because it was such a dominant maritime power. It had also developed an efficient ability to administer and govern its own (and other) people. The Industrial Revolution gave it the motivation to look for new markets to trade with.

The English People Today

In the late 1950s and early 1960s, there was a shortage of labor in Britain for low-paid jobs. The government encouraged people from British Commonwealth countries (countries formerly under direct government control from England) to come to Britain to increase the labor force. Afro-Caribbean and Asian immigrants arrived in large numbers, settling mainly in and around large towns and cities. It was the first experience that most white British people had of living with people of different races. Racial tensions erupted. There were race riots in London in 1958. The Afro-Caribbean and Asian people in England today, many of whom are now the second generation to be born in England, still live in and around the larger towns and cities. Rural England remains largely white, Anglo-Saxon territory, as it has been for the last 1,500 years.

Despite the construction of the Channel Tunnel between England and continental Europe, the English (and other Brits) remain true to their island character as different from the rest of Europe. The English (and all British) people today enjoy democratic freedom, cultural diversity, high standards of living, and social institutions to protect their well-being. England has not been invaded by a foreign power since William the Conqueror in 1066. The last revolution in England was in 1688, when James II (1633–1701) was overthrown and forced into exile because of his pro-Catholic policies. For more than 300 years, despite some difficult and traumatic episodes, the country and its people have benefited from a relatively peaceful and stable evolution. The uninterrupted continuity of that evolution has preserved the traditions and culture that have molded the character of the English people.

THE LANGUAGES OF ENGLAND

3

From Old English to Modern English

English is the language not only of England but of the whole British Isles, North America (except Quebec), Australia, New Zealand, and many other countries that used to be part of the British Empire (including India, South Africa, and many West Indian islands, for example). At the beginning of the twenty-first century, it is estimated that English as a person's first language is spoken by more than 400 million people around the world. Even more than that—estimated at 500 million to as many as 1 billion—have learned English as a foreign language. In the time of Queen Elizabeth I, the Americas were only just becoming settled by English and European people. By 2001, there were approximately 284 million people in the United States alone, of whom about 240 million spoke English as their first language. It is estimated that 5 to 10 percent of the population of India—from 50 to 100 million people, more than the population of the entire United Kingdom—are fluent in English. English is now much more than the language of its single mother country. It is one of the dominant languages of the planet.

From Old to Modern English

Humans have lived in England for at least 50,000 years. The language those first inhabitants spoke was not written down. The Celts, who arrived in Britain soon

Pictured at left is a stained-glass window depicting King Arthur being advised by his magical teacher, Merlin. Pictured above is a collection of English newspapers featuring headlines about soccer player David Beckham's 2003 four-year contract with Real Madrid. Beckham is considered one of the most popular sports figures in the world.

after 700 BC, were the first people whose language we know about today. Welsh, Gaelic, and Cornish are Celtic languages still spoken in the British Isles. Celtic influence on the English language, however, was very slight. The Celtic influence is largely found in place-names. Thames, for example, is the Celtic name for the river that runs through London. The name London itself was probably the name of a Celtic tribe. Celtic words for river or water survive as place-names, such as the town (and river) Avon, the river Exe (and city of Exeter), and the town of Dover. The Angles, Saxons, Jutes, and later the Scandinavians (Vikings) invaded and conquered the Celts. The Romans pushed the Celtic speaking population from the east to the far west of the country. Anglo-Saxon tribes invaded the east of Britain after the Romans left in AD 410. Because of the distance between Celts and Anglo-Saxons, there was very little mixing of Celtic and Anglo-Saxon languages, which were the origins of modern English. The only places in the British Isles where Celtic languages are still widely spoken today are along the western fringes (Ireland, the Western Isles of Scotland, and Wales).

The Latin language was a different matter. Latin was introduced into Britain when the Romans invaded and settled after AD 55. Latin was the language of the Roman Empire, which was feared but also respected, even after its downfall in the fifth century AD. Anglo-Saxon tribes invaded England from around AD 700. Latin was the language they knew from contact with the Romans on the European continent. Latin was the symbol of power, relating to both the military and, later, to religious matters. In AD 597, Pope Gregory sent a monk named Augustine (along

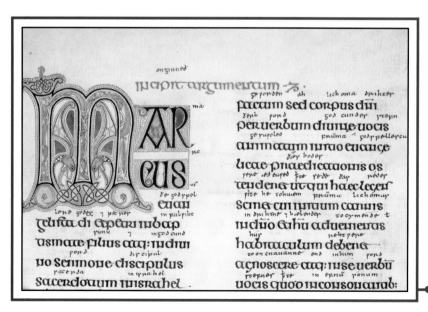

This is an early (circa AD 698) Latin text of the Gospel of Saint Mark from the New Testament. Before the printing press, scribes spent years copying the Bible using precise and decorative scripts.

with about forty other monks) to convert the Anglo-Saxons in England to Christianity. By AD 700, all of England was Christian.

In those times, the Christian church in England was the intellectual center of Europe. The language of the church, and of the Roman civilization which so influenced English culture, was Latin. This is the reason why so many Latin influences appear in the vocabulary of Old English.

Old English

There are three stages of evolution of the English language: Old English (approximately AD 450–1150), Middle English (1150–1500), and Modern English (1500 to the present day). The beginnings of Old English date from when the first Germanic tribes—the Jutes, Angles, and Saxons—invaded Britain in the fifth century. The Old English

---

This brief extract shows written Old English:

> *Wæs he se mon in weoruldhade geseted*
> *oô pa tide pe he wæs gelyfdre ylde,*
> *ond næfre nænig leoô geleornode.*
> *Ond he forpon oft in gebeorscipe,*
> *ponne pær wæs blisse intinga gedemed,*
> *pæt heo ealle sceolden purh*
> *endebyrdnesse be hearpan singan.*

Translation:
"He was a man settled in the secular [non-religious] life until he was of an advanced age; and he had never learned any poems. He therefore found himself at a banquet, when there was to be a time of joyfulness, and they all had to take it in turns to sing with the harp."

—*From a late ninth-century Old English translation of the* Ecclesiastical History of the English Nation, *written in Latin by the Venerable Bede, describing the life of the poet Caedmon, around* AD 731

spoken by those people was almost purely Germanic. It had very few words derived from Latin and none derived from French. Almost all the English words derived from French and Latin came into the English language in the Middle English period or later. Today, those words make up more than half of all common English words.

The names England and English emerged in the Old English period. The invading Germanic tribes were called either Angles or Saxons, or just Anglo-Saxons, referring to all the tribes. Somewhere between AD 650 and 700, Latin writers called them all just *Angli* or *Anglia*. Even before that, however, the language of all the Germanic invaders was called *Englisc* (pronounced "English"), from the Old English name for the Angles, *Engle*. From around the year 1000, the name *Englaland* ("land of the Angles") was used as the name of the country inhabited by the Angles, Saxons, and all the other invading Germanic tribes. So, the name for the language (Englisc) is older than the name for the country (Englaland).

Danish (Viking) raiders started attacking the east coast of England in the year 797. Over the next 200 years, they settled in an area that came to be known as the Danelaw, which was most of northeast England. Today, the northeast of England has more than 1,500 place-names from the Old Norse language spoken by the Vikings. More than 600 place-names end in "-by," the Danish word for "town" or "farm" (Derby, Rugby, and Grimsby, for example). Many others end in "-thorp(e)" (Althorp, Linthorpe, and so on), meaning "village"; "-thwaite" (Braithwaite, Applethwaite, and so on), meaning "clearing"; or "-toft" (Lowestoft, Eastoft, and so on), meaning "homestead." In Old English, the word *sindon* means "are" (as in "we are"). In fact, "are" is the Old Norse form of the verb "to be." It replaced the Old English form "sindon" and is, of course, still used today.

From Middle to Modern English

In the Middle English period, thousands of English words derived from Latin and French replaced Old English Germanic words. Only about 15 percent of the original Old English vocabulary has survived, alongside the same or similar words derived from Latin and French. Modern English, for example, has the words "ask," "question," and "interrogate," which all mean approximately the same thing. The first is from Old English, the second from French, and the third from Latin. There are thousands of other English words meaning the same thing from the three different origins. This is one reason why English has a larger vocabulary than other languages: it has more roots in many other languages. Middle English is much easier for us to read than Old English. Nearly half of all the words in Modern English came from Latin or French words that entered the English language in the Middle English period.

William the Conqueror invaded England in 1066. Because he was French, he appointed many French-speaking barons, bishops, and abbots to positions of authority in England. French words gradually came into the English language, mixing with the Old English still spoken by most people. French was used mainly by people at the royal court or in high government positions.

A sixteenth-century engraving of John Wycliffe. Before Wycliffe's English translation, only members of the clergy who knew Latin were able to read scripture.

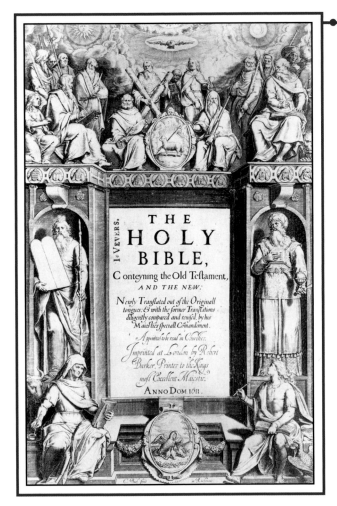

The original title page of the King James Version of the New Testament. English artist Robert Barker printed this page in London in 1611.

English, however, continued to be the main language spoken by the common people. In 1362, English was used for the first time at the opening of Parliament. John Wycliffe (1330–1384) translated the Bible from Latin into English (known as the Wycliffe Bible) between 1380 and 1384, so it could be read by everyone. He used about 1,000 new English words derived from Latin. After the Hundred Years' War (1337–1453) against France, English nationalism confirmed the dominance of the English language. By the early 1400s, it was widely used in writing and speech. By 1500, English had become the popular language of the country.

When William Caxton (1422?–1491) set up the first printing press in London in 1477, there were still many dialects of English used around the country. Other publishers followed Caxton's example. Within about 100 years, the standard English used in printed books could be understood throughout the country. William Shakespeare (1564–1616) wrote in a language that can easily be understood today. The King James Bible (the Authorized Version of the Bible), published in 1611, was a translation of earlier English-language Bibles. The aim of the translators was to improve earlier English translations and to make "one principall good one" that could be read easily by everyone. In 1755, Samuel Johnson (1709–1784) completed his great *Dictionary of the English Language,* which "conferred [gave] stability" to the language. That stability guided the English language toward the Modern English that we speak today and that continues to evolve.

This is the title page of Volume I of the first English dictionary, which was published in 1755. Samuel Johnson used quotations from English literature (from writers such as Shakespeare and Milton) to better illustrate the definitions of the words.

A

DICTIONARY

OF THE

ENGLISH LANGUAGE:

IN WHICH

The WORDS are deduced from their ORIGINALS,

AND

ILLUSTRATED in their DIFFERENT SIGNIFICATIONS

BY

EXAMPLES from the best WRITERS.

TO WHICH ARE PREFIXED,

A HISTORY of the LANGUAGE,

AND

An ENGLISH GRAMMAR.

BY SAMUEL JOHNSON, A.M.

IN TWO VOLUMES.

VOL. I.

LONDON,

Printed by W. STRAHAN,

For J. and P. KNAPTON; T. and T. LONGMAN; C. HITCH and L. HAWES;
A. MILLAR; and R. and J. DODSLEY.

MDCCLV.

The Languages of England

Most people in England speak English, but not everyone does. Some first-generation Asian immigrants have still not learned English. Many others speak English as a second language, alongside their mother tongues (Hindi, Urdu, or Gujarat, to name just a few from the Indian subcontinent). Immigrants from Asia in particular, but also from former British Empire countries in Africa (Nigeria, Gambia, and Kenya, for example), have brought dozens of "imported" languages to England over the past century. These other languages were originally just spoken in pockets in the larger towns and cities. Now, the British-born second and third generations of those original immigrant communities are more widespread. They make up only 2 to 3 percent of the English population, but they reflect a linguistic diversity that was absent for most of England's history.

Cornish

Cornish is the only true "other" language spoken in England. It is an old Gaelic language that used to be spoken in Cornwall, in the far west of England. The language is called Kernewek in Cornish. It is a direct descendant of the languages spoken in Britain by the early Celts, from around 700 BC. By AD 1200, Cornish was the common language of Cornwall. By 1600, it was only spoken in western Cornwall. It ceased to be a native spoken language with the death of the last native speaker, Dolly Pentreath, in 1777. Interest in the language never died, however, and there has been an attempt to revive it since the beginning of the twentieth century. Several thousand people have now learned to speak Cornish, but there are probably no more than a hundred or so fluent speakers.

A man on his way home from work buys a copy of the *Evening Standard*. People who sell the *Evening Standard* on the streets are well known in London for their loud voices and cockney accents. To advertise the newspaper the street sellers yell "Eein Stannard!" (*Evening Standard*) at passersby.

Regional Differences

Throughout England people speak English with different accents. There are also regional dialects, which are different ways of speaking the English language. Regional dialects have been diluted or lost altogether by the widespread use of standard English (sometimes called received pronunciation) in television and radio broadcasting. Since the late 1980s, the kind of English spoken around London, so-called estuary English (from the estuary of the river Thames), has become fashionable, as received pronunciation has gone out of fashion. Estuary English is a working-class regional accent.

In England, an accent or way of speaking can identify the speaker's social class (lower, middle, or upper) almost as easily as it can identify his or her geographical origin. One particular way of speaking that identifies a person as upper class is the use of "one" for "I." The following quote from a newspaper interview with a famous English explorer is a good example of this: "'It was a dramatic meeting in unknown Africa,' he told me years later, 'yet I never considered failure. One merely assumed one would be successful and, as it turned out, one was.'"

Many places also have different dialect words and phrases that are still commonly used. Some examples from Cornwall in the southwest and from Yorkshire in the north appear below.

Cornwall

Bee nor baw: Keeping silent. "She never said bee nor baw."
Cab: Mishandle or disturb. "Don't cab that cat, now!"
Dreckly: Soon. "I'll be coming, dreckly, soon as I finish this work."

Yorkshire

Ax: To ask. "Go ax the copper [policeman] t'way [the way]."
Owt: Anything. "Have ye got owt for me?"

Cockney Rhyming Slang

Traditionally, a Cockney was anyone born within the sound of the ringing bells of St.-Mary-le-Bow Church in the East End of London. Cockney rhyming slang originated among Cockneys, probably around the start of the twentieth century. It replaces a particular word with a phrase or other words that rhyme with it. The slang might have started as a code among criminals in the East End to pass on secret information. It later became adopted by ordinary people as a humorous way of talking, without any criminal or secret intent. Cockney rhyming slang is most genuine when it is spoken by a true Cockney or at least by someone with a true Cockney accent. There are thousands of expressions used in Cockney rhyming slang. Some of the more common ones are as follows:

bottle and stopper: Copper (policeman). "Oi, George! Look out for the bottle and stopper, will ya?"
currant bun (a kind of raisin muffin): Sun or son. "Cor, blimey, George! Looks like you stayed out too long in the old currant bun!"
on and off: Cough. "That's a terrible on and off you got there, George."
rhythm and blues: Shoes. "Blimey, George! Look at the price of them rhythm and blues!"
tin of beans: Jeans. "Oi, George! Where'd you get them tin of beans?"

ENGLISH MYTHS AND LEGENDS

4

nglish myths and legends come from two main sources: history and people's imaginations. The most famous legendary figures, such as King Arthur and Robin Hood, have some connection with historical fact. Through the ages, the imagination of storytellers, writers, and poets has transformed what might have been real people originally into the legends that we know today. Superstitions about goblins, miracles, and devils emerged in times when most people were illiterate and simple peasants. As a substitute for knowledge, they created myths and beliefs to explain the world around them.

King Arthur

King Arthur is the central figure of England's most famous legend. We do not know for sure if King Arthur was a real person. He might have been a Celtic warrior king of the fifth or sixth century who fought against the Saxons. Many places around Britain claim to be his birthplace. Tintagel, in Cornwall, with its early Celtic connections, seems to be the most popular choice. The original medieval authors of the Arthurian legends began writing about him in the ninth and tenth centuries. They knew the stories of King Arthur handed down from earlier times.

Pictured at left is a statue of King Arthur from 1513. The statue shows the legendary Arthur in medieval armor. This statue was cast by Peter Vischer for the tomb of Holy Roman Emperor Maximillian I. Pictured above is a page from *Lancelot du Lac*, a 1490 French telling of the Arthurian legends. The image depicts Arthur with his knights of the Round Table.

Arthur Hunt made this watercolor of the village of Tintagel on the rocky coast of Cornwall in 1887. Tintagel Castle is the supposed birthplace of King Arthur.

They used those stories to create an imaginary world of magic, adventure, chivalry (honor), and mystery. Whatever the reality of Arthur was, the legends were pure fantasies of imagination.

Geoffrey of Monmouth (1100–1155) wrote a famous book, *The History of the Kings of Britain,* in 1136. This "history" is a fantasy in which the first complete story of Arthur's life appears. According to Geoffrey, Arthur's father, Uther, fell in love with Ygerna, the wife of Gorlois, the Duke of Cornwall. Gorlois realized this and locked Ygerna away in his castle at Tintagel. Merlin the magician offered to turn Uther into a replica of Gorlois so he could get into the castle to be with Ygerna. As a result of this deception, Ygerna had a son, Arthur. When Uther died, Arthur became king. He fought against the Saxons, as well as the Picts in the north, the Irish, the Romans in Gaul (France), and others. He married Guinevere and formed a group of knights who would later become the knights of the Round Table. Geoffrey does not include a round table in his account. That was a later addition to the legend. The royal court at Camelot was also a later invention by other writers. Geoffrey wrote a separate story about Merlin, *The Life of Merlin,* around 1151. Merlin was Arthur's court magician, prophet, and adviser throughout Arthur's life, according to Geoffrey.

Geoffrey writes that Arthur was wounded in battle against his traitor nephew, Mordred. Merlin took Arthur to the magical island of Avalon to be attended to. But Geoffrey never mentions that Arthur died. This is a central feature of the legend: that

Arthur never actually died and that one day he will return to rule his kingdom. Later writers introduced other characters and themes into the Arthur legend, including the adulterous love of Sir Lancelot for Arthur's wife, Guinevere, contrasted with the pure love of Lancelot's illegitimate son, Sir Galahad; Galahad's search for the Holy Grail; Arthur drawing the magical sword called Excalibur from a rock to win his throne and become king; the Lady of the Lake giving Excalibur to Arthur; and the round table that Arthur makes for the knights of his court so all of them can sit around it as equals. New details and stories about the legend of King Arthur have been created from the twelfth century to the present day. They include the 1960s stage musical and movie *Camelot* and even the satirical movie *Monty Python and the Holy Grail* in 1975.

Robin Hood

Everyone knows the legend of Robin Hood: the outlaw who robbed from the rich and gave to the poor; his band of merry men who lived with him in Sherwood Forest; his love for Maid Marian; and his enemy, the Sheriff of Nottingham. Rhymes about Robin Hood go back to the fourteenth century. Thirty-eight original ballads about Robin Hood, from the fifteenth to the seventeenth centuries, still exist. Each one tells a slightly different version of the Robin Hood story. None gives any reason why he became an outlaw. Unlike King Arthur, Robin Hood is described in the ballads as a real person, "a good yeoman [an ordinary man],"

An illustration from *Robin Hood and His Life in the Merry Greenwood* shows the fight between Robin Hood and Little John. The book was written by Rose Yeatman Woolf in 1910.

whose "love for Our dear Lady [the Virgin Mary] kept him from deadly sin." Included in his band of merry men in the wood are Little John (who was huge), Friar Tuck (a monk who liked fighting and hunting), Will Scathlock, and Much, the miller's son (the latter being two of Robin's most trusted companions). Maid Marian began to appear in the ballads as Robin's sweetheart starting around 1500. Robin, the rebel hero, fights against authority figures but is generous to good fellows, whatever their rank. His view is well described in the following verses from the ballad "A Little Geste of Robin Hood," from the early sixteenth century (modernized by Richard Barber in his book *Myths and Legends of the British Isles*):

> "We shall do well," said Robin,
> "If we together stand;
> Though look you harm no farmer
> That tills with plough the land.
> Nor shall you harm a yeoman
> That through the greenwood goes;
> Nor shall you harm nor knight nor squire
> If they are good fellows.
> The bishops and archbishops—
> Them shall you beat and bind:
> Let the high sheriff of Nottingham
> Be foremost in your mind."

Dick Whittington

The popular story of Dick Whittington and his cat is a myth. The story goes that, in the reign of Edward III (1312–1377), Dick was a poor orphan employed as a kitchen boy in a big London house. He was badly treated by the other servants and ran away. As he rested by a milestone, he heard the ringing bells of St.-Mary-le-Bow Church in the East End of London. The bells seemed to be saying, "Turn again, Whittington, Lord Mayor of London." He returned to his master's home. The master, who was rich, offered all his servants the opportunity to contribute something

Pictured at right is a painting of Dick Whittington and his fortunate feline taking a break on their way to London. The illustration was done by Frank Adams and was published in a collection of fables and legends called *My Nursery Storybook*.

Henry Liverseege (1803–1832) painted the lively Friar Tuck, one of Robin Hood's merry men, raising his glass for a toast.

toward a trading voyage by one of his ships. Dick put up his cat as his share in the voyage. On the North African coast, a local king paid a large amount of money for Dick's cat to get rid of a plague of rats. That money became the source of Dick's fortune. Dick married his master's daughter and became lord mayor of London three times. Whittington was actually Richard Whittington, the son of a Gloucestershire knight. Whittington inherited his father's fortune and opened a store in London that sold expensive cloth and clothing to wealthy Londoners. He entered politics and was sheriff of London from 1393 to 1394 and lord mayor of London three times (1397–1398, 1406–1407, and 1419–1420). He died childless in 1423 and left his fortune to charities.

Saints and Miracles

The most famous of all English saints is Saint George, now the patron saint of England. Nothing is known for sure about the man, but his origins lie in Turkey and the Middle East. He was originally linked with the first Christian Crusades against the Muslims in the eleventh and into the thirteenth centuries. Other sources claim he was a Roman soldier who was executed in the fourth century for protesting against the Roman emperor Diocletian's persecution of Christians. Throughout the Christian world, Saint George is honored for his courage in defense of the Christian church and for the miraculous deeds he performed. The banner of Saint George is the red cross of a martyr (one who dies for a cause) on a white background. It became used by English soldiers possibly in the reign of Richard I (Richard the Lionheart; 1157–1199). Ever since, it has been the symbol of a crusader who fights in the name of the Christian church. The legend of Saint George slaying a dragon to save the life of a princess first appears in the *Legenda Aurea* (Golden Legend), from 1265. In a later work, *The Famous History of the Seven Champions of Christendom*

(1596–1597), George is said to have been born in England. He slays a dragon to save an Egyptian princess. After being poisoned by another dragon, he is buried at St. George's Chapel in Windsor Castle, one of the castles of England's kings and queens. In 1348, Edward III created the Order of the Knights of the Garter, the highest honor that can be awarded to an individual by a British monarch. St. George's Chapel is the seat of the order, and Saint George is its patron.

Paolo Uccello painted *Saint George and the Dragon* around 1470. According to one legend, a dragon terrorized a pagan village that sacrificed its people to please the dragon. Saint George rescued a princess from the dragon and offered to slay it if the townspeople agreed to become Christians.

Many places in England are named after saints or miracles. The town of St. Albans, for example, just north of London, was called Verulamium in Roman and Saxon times. According to the early English historian the Venerable Bede, a man called Alban, a citizen of the town, was executed there in the year 304 because he gave shelter to a Christian priest. For that, he became Saint Alban. About 500 years later, the English king Offa had a miraculous vision. The vision directed him to seek out the body of Saint Alban and build a monastery at that place. He went to Verulamium, found Saint Alban's relics, and built a church there. The town has been called St. Albans ever since.

In Somerset (western England), there is a town called Keynsham. The name is said to derive from the fifth-century saint, Kenya, who lived there. The place was infested with snakes. According to legend, Saint Kenya turned all the snakes to stone. All the stones around the town are said to have witnessed this miracle.

The town of Bury St. Edmunds in Suffolk is named after Saint Edmund, a king of the Angles. He was defeated by the Danes (Vikings) near a place called Hoxne in Suffolk and hid under a bridge to get away. A newly married couple crossing the bridge saw him. They betrayed him to his enemies. When he was captured, he cursed anyone going to get married who crossed the bridge. Edmund was killed by the Danes and became a martyr because he would not deny his Christian faith. His body lay at Hoxne for many years. Then it was taken to be buried at a place called Beodricsweorth (BED-ricks-worth), which was renamed Bury St. Edmunds.

The Giants of Albion

This is the legend of how the first people who came to England were giants and why the country came to be called Albion. According to a thirteenth-century story, in 3970 BC, a king in Greece had thirty daughters. The eldest was named Albina. The daughters agreed secretly never to be under the control of anyone, including their husbands, whom they plotted to kill. For his daughters' treachery, the king sent them into exile. By ship they reached a distant land. Albina was the first to step on shore, so she called the land Albion. After a while, the daughters were made pregnant by evil beings called incubi, who took on human forms. The daughters' children were giants and ruled Albion until invaders came to the land in 1136 BC. One of the invaders, Brutus, overthrew all the giants except for one called Gogmagog, who was 20 feet (6.1 m) tall. Gogmagog told Brutus how all his ancestors had come to that land. Brutus changed the name of the land from Albion to the name we call it today: Britain.

This is a nineteenth-century drawing of the giant Gogmagog. Gogmagog is often depicted as a protector and gatekeeper of London.

This panel of drawings illustrates different types of devils. The page is from *Sadducismus Triumphatus, Part II*, a 1682 book by Joseph Glanvill.

Demons and Goblins

In English legends, the devil is sometimes an evil destroyer, sometimes a stupid failure, and sometimes an enemy defeated by humans. Features of the local landscape said to be made by the devil are usually things like rocks, boulders, or stony ground. In legends in which the devil brings sinners to justice, he is seen as the instrument of God's judgment. The expression, "Well, speak of the devil!" about someone who arrives by coincidence as they are being talked about, is an abbreviation of the proverb, "Talk of the devil and he will appear."

Dozens of places around England have legends related to the devil. In Kirby Lonsdale, in the north of England, for example, Devil's Bridge goes over the river Lune. The devil was said to have built the bridge one night so that an old woman farmer could retrieve her cow that had wandered off to the other side of the river. As a favor in return, the devil asked to carry off the first living thing that crossed the bridge. The next morning, the old woman came to the bridge with a dog hidden under her cloak. She threw food onto the bridge, and the dog ran over to eat it. Cheated by the woman's trick, the devil clawed at one of the stones on the bridge's arch before disappearing. The marks of the devil's claw are still there. There is also a pile of stones near the bridge. These stones are said to have been left over from the load of rocks the devil carried in his apron to build the bridge.

Depending on their nature and where they are found, hobgoblins in England are called goblins, hobs (in the north), brownies, pixies, or pucks. Goblins are usually mischievous and sometimes kindly. Brownies are useful. In Yorkshire, Hob's Hole cave was the home of a goblin called Hob Thrush, who cured whooping cough. A parent would take his or her sick child into the cave and say the words, "Hobhole Hob! My bairn's [child's] gotten t' kink-cough [whooping cough]. Tak't off! Tak't off! [Take it away!]"

ENGLISH FESTIVALS AND CEREMONIES OF ANTIQUITY AND TODAY

5

There are many fairs and festivals in England. Some are ancient. Some celebrate the seasons. Some, like the great music festivals, have an international reputation. Others are very strange events based on traditions whose origins have long since been forgotten. Summer is the great festival time in England, when the weather is best for outdoor events. The most common festivals in England are the local village fetes (*fête* means "festival" in French) held by towns and villages all around the country from May through September. The most spectacular are the huge pop-music festivals that attract hundreds of thousands of people over several days.

Arts and Music Festivals

The Glyndebourne Festival (May to August) is England's premier classical music event. It started in 1934 after John Cristie built a small opera house for his opera-singing wife on the grounds of their home at Glyndebourne in East Sussex, just north of Brighton. The original small opera house was replaced by a large structure in 1992. The festival attracts well-established opera singers, set designers, and conductors from around the world. Spectators are free to wander around the grounds of Glyndebourne and often set out elaborate picnics as part of the festival atmosphere. The Cheltenham International Music Festival is held in July at

Pictured at left, the Chiddingfold Bonfire lights up the night sky. Once a small village celebration, the event now attracts around 10,000 celebrants each year. The Chiddingfold Bonfire is part of the Guy Fawkes Day celebrations on November 5. Pictured above, singers and musicians perform at the Aldeburgh Festival of Music. The festival was founded in 1948 by British composer Benjamin Britten.

Cheltenham, near Gloucester (GLOSS-ter), northwest of Oxford. It is mainly a festival of classical music, but has fringe events of jazz, folk, and world music, as well as theater and comedy. The Aldeburgh Festival in June is a showcase of classical music at the old Suffolk town of Aldeburgh on the east coast. In July 2003, the York Early Music Festival in the north of England featured music from the twelfth to the eighteenth centuries. London hosts various summer arts festivals, including London International Festival of Theatre (every two years), London Festival of Baroque Music (June), and the Spitalfields Festival (June) for early classical and world music.

There are numerous outdoor pop-music festivals in England. The biggest is probably the Glastonbury Festival, held on the last weekend of June at Pilton, near Glastonbury in the west of England. This event, like Woodstock in New York, is as famous for the mud and crowds it usually produces as it is for the dozens of pop-music bands it attracts. The pop-music festivals on the Isle of Wight (mid-June) and at Reading (late August) are now as famous (and as crowded) as Glastonbury. These original events have spawned dozens of other pop-music festivals around the country.

The Hay-on-Wye Festival in May and June is the premier international literary festival in England. The Swindon Festival of Literature, at Swindon in the west of England, is held in early May. Literary festivals are sometimes held in conjunction with music and other arts events. The Bath Literature Festival runs just before the town's International Music Festival in May. The Canterbury Festival in October has a variety of music, dance, drama, and film, as well as talks and sessions dedicated to literature.

Folk Festivals

The Notting Hill Carnival in London is Europe's biggest outdoor street festival and second in the world only to the Carnival of Rio de Janeiro. The Notting Hill Carnival is held on the last weekend of August. Notting Hill used to be one of the main Afro-Caribbean immigrant areas of London. The carnival still has a mainly Caribbean feel, even though Notting Hill itself has become a trendy and fashionable (and expensive) place to live. Colorful floats and costumed dancers, parades, loud music, ethnic food stalls, and huge crowds characterize the carnival. A more conservative event is the Cheltenham Folk Festival, in Gloucestershire, northwest of London, in February. The festival features folk music and drama by British and international folk artists. Near Bournemouth on the south coast, the Wimborne Folk Festival is held at Wimborne Minster over three days in June. It features folk music and dance competitions. Although not strictly a folk "festival," the summer solstice (either June 21 or 22) celebrated at Stonehenge every year is a truly folk English tradition. Druids (pagan priests) and nature-loving ordinary people gather near Stonehenge before dawn on the summer solstice as a form of midsummer ritual of pagan worship. Stonehenge has been a place of mystery, spirituality, and folklore for thousands of years.

A Caribbean dancer is dressed in a colorful costume at the Notting Hill Carnival. The festival begins with Panorama, a steel drum competition. Calypso music is a major part of the festival.

This nineteenth-century Italian print depicts Stonehenge as it might have looked in prehistoric times.

Harvest festivals and May Day are among the best-known festivals. There are many traditional customs around harvesttime, but harvest festivals in England relate specifically to the church and schools. Food is donated to schools and churches around the country. Prayers and sermons of thanks are given. The food is then distributed to the poor. A vicar in Cornwall invented this kind of festival in 1843. Earlier harvest festivals had involved great suppers for the farmworkers, including excessive eating and drinking.

May Day festivals celebrating the beginning of summer date back to medieval times or even earlier. "Bringing in the may" is the tradition of going out into the countryside on the first day of May to pick flowers and greenery and bringing it all back to the village to decorate the church and public places. In the nineteenth and early twentieth centuries, children made garlands of flowers and visited local houses, singing songs to collect money. Maypoles, dating back to the fourteenth century, are the most traditional symbol of May Day celebrations. The pole was set up at the center of the community. People danced around it and hung garlands on it. The custom of weaving ribbons around the pole by the dancers only started in the nineteenth century.

England has other rather stranger local folk festivals. The Straw Bear festival is celebrated in the southeast flatlands of Cambridgeshire, particularly in the town of Whittlesey. The festival originally celebrated Plough Monday, the first Monday after Twelfth Day (January 6). Farmworkers in the Cambridgeshire area returned to work on Plough Monday after the Christmas holidays. That day, a man or boy would be dressed in straw to look like a bear. He would be led by a rope to perform for money like a dancing bear in front of wealthy people's houses. Local police abolished

Women in white dresses dance around the maypole on May 1, 1948. Today celebrants aren't typically separated by gender.

the custom in 1909. In 1980, a local man revived the custom at Whittlesey as a local mini–folk festival. Villagers paint their faces green and black for the event. Other folk events, such as Morris dancing (see chapter 8), are included in the festivities. Cheese rolling takes place at an annual festival in late May at the very steep Cooper's Hill, near Brockworth, Gloucestershire. A 7-pound (3.1-kilogram) round of double Gloucester cheese is rolled down the hill. People chase after it. Whoever gets to the cheese first wins it. There are several races, one of which is for women only. The origins of this quaint English custom are unknown today.

Another curious English folk custom is gurning. People compete to pull the funniest looking or most contorted face. Gurning competitions used to be popular at fairs and festivals all around the country. The only regularly held event today (the World Champion Gurning Competition) is at the Egremont Crab-Apple Fair. This fair, at Egremont in northern England, has apparently been held every year since it started in 1267 (except during the two world wars). Apart from its gurning contest, the fair has also a pipe-smoking contest, a sentimental song-singing competition, and other odd events.

There are a number of festivals in England in which participants dress up in historical costume to reenact a particular battle or period of English history. The Tewkesbury Medieval Festival in July is held at Tewkesbury, Gloucestershire. Around 800 people dress up in medieval clothing to reenact the Battle of Tewkesbury in 1471. Guy Fawkes Night marks the failure of the plot lead by Guy Fawkes to blow up Parliament and King James I in 1605. To commemorate the failed plot, every November 5 (and for weeks before that), fireworks are set off and bonfires are burned around the country. Children make stuffed effigies (big dolls) of Guy Fawkes (called the Guy), set them up in a public place, and ask people passing by for money ("Penny for the Guy?"). Most of the fireworks now are set off in public displays.

A production of Mozart's *Cosí Fan Tutte* is performed at an operatic music festival. The opera tells the story of two men who swap fiancées to test their loyalty.

Sporting and Other Festivals

The most well known sporting festivals in England are the Cheltenham Festival and the Henley Royal Regatta. Cheltenham is a weeklong series of important horse races and a highly social event. The Henley Royal Regatta is a series of rowing events on the Thames at Henley. Hundreds of races are rowed by dozens of teams from around the world. Like Cheltenham, the event is a great social event as well as a sporting occasion. There are also a number of important garden shows during the year. The biggest are the Chelsea Flower Show in London, in May, and the Hampton Court Flower Show at Hampton Court, just outside London, in July.

Village Fetes and Fairs

Most villages and small towns around England have their own fetes during the spring and summer months. These are usually one-day affairs. The local people set up exhibits, food stalls, and attractions for children at the town hall or on a local village green (the little park at the center of many English villages). Fetes are mainly a way of getting the community together. There are competitions for the best agricultural produce (flowers, fruit, and vegetables). Secondhand books and clothes are for sale, as are freshly baked goods. In many village festivals, there is music and dancing. If the fete is on the village green or in a nearby field, there might also be a *gymkhana* (horse-riding competition) and other sporting competitions.

At the 1995 Henley Royal Regatta, a rowing team presses on to the finish. Henley-on-Thames is a small town, but is well known for its rowing. The regatta attracts thousands to Henley each year.

English Festivals and Ceremonies of Antiquity and Today

Flower lovers gather at the annual Chelsea Flower Show in London. The flower show is organized by the Royal Horticulture Society and is held every May.

Town fairs in England are an ancient tradition dating back to pre-Christian times. The early Christian church converted pagan festivals into feast days of Christian worship. After the religious ceremony, the people would set up booths and stalls to trade their goods, often within the churchyard itself. Once a fair had been running some years, it could be established by law as a commercial event by getting a royal charter from the king or queen. Merchants sold all kinds of wares at these fairs, from horses, cattle, and sheep to cloth, hats, and cheese. Scarborough Fair, on the Yorkshire coast, was given a royal charter by Henry III in 1253. Traders from all over Europe brought their goods to trade for English wool, leather, grain, and craft items over forty-five days in August and September. Minstrels, jugglers, dancers, and fortune-tellers entertained the crowds. The fair died out in around 1788. There were some specialized fairs, such as the Barnet and Morley Horse Fairs, the Frome Cheese Fair, and the Nottingham Goose Fair.

There were also "mop" (hiring) fairs. Servants at these fairs would stand in a row wearing or holding some symbol of their trade—a bit of straw for a cowherd, a tuft of wool for a shepherd, a mop for a cleaning lady. On being hired for a year's work, they were usually given a "fasten-penny" (a little money to close the deal), and then went off to enjoy the fair for the rest of the day.

Another form of town fairs were wakes. Wakes, especially in the north of England, were really holiday times for the people of the town. In fact, they were the main holiday of the year and could run for up to four days. Wakes were originally feast days held to commemorate the town's patron saint, as distinct from the chartered commercial fairs. St. Giles Fair in Oxford is one of the largest surviving wake fairs. It was first mentioned in 1625 as "a small parish festival." In Elizabethan times, it became a market fair. Now it is mainly a festival of fun and entertainment.

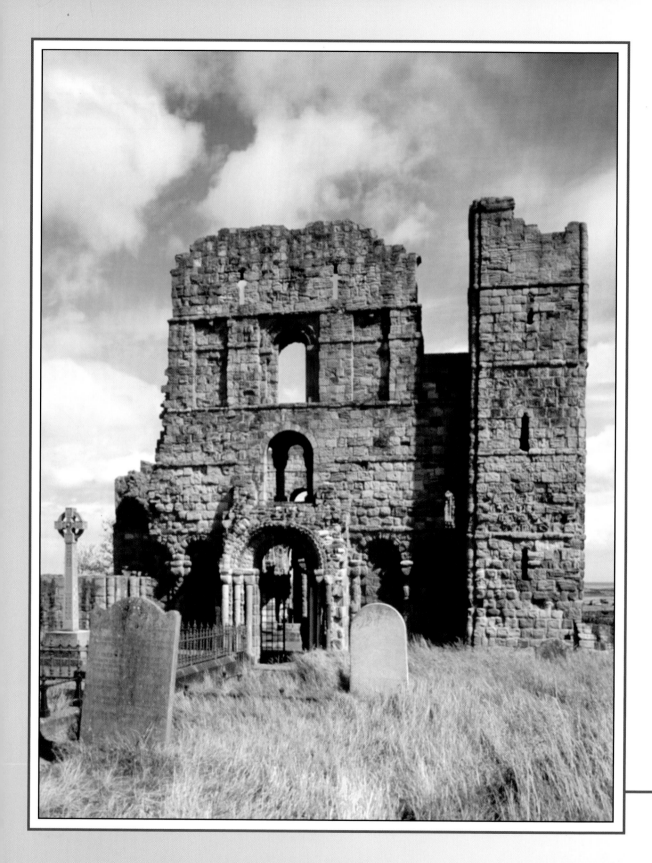

THE RELIGIONS OF ENGLAND THROUGHOUT HISTORY

6

The church is one of England's great institutions. A typical view of the English countryside includes church steeples rising above the roofs of surrounding houses. The different styles of English church steeples reflect all the ages of English history, from Saxon to modern times. The sound of church bells ringing belongs not just to English religious tradition but to the English landscape. Hymns sung in English churches come from some of the greatest English poets and composers. The photograph of St. Paul's Cathedral in London, surrounded but unharmed by the devastation of German bombing (the blitzkrieg, or "lightning war") in World War II, reminds the English of their indomitable spirit.

Despite all those reminders of their Christian faith, the English are not a particularly religious people. In 2001, just over two-thirds of the English population described themselves as practicing Christians. (Almost 15 percent of the population claimed they had no religion.) The Bible is still a best-seller: more than 1 million copies are sold every year in Britain. Around 80 percent of all couples that marry in England do so in a religious ceremony. And yet, the English are a rather secular (nonreligious) people. Fewer than 50 percent of the population

Pictured at left are the ruins of the monastery at Lindisfarne Priory (also known as Holy Island). The monastery was founded by Saint Aidan, who used it as a base for mission work in England during the fifth century. Pictured above is a Saxon church and cemetery in Norfolk.

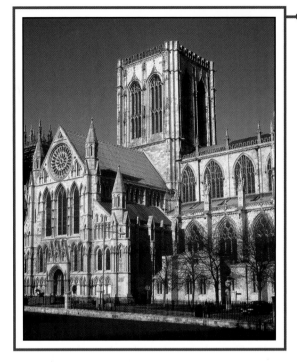

Yorkminster dominates the town of York. It is the largest Gothic cathedral in northern Europe. Work began on the cathedral in 1220, but was not completed until 1472.

claim to believe in God. For most English people, church is more of a social event—an institution—than a sacred place of worship and prayer. Fewer than 10 percent of the population regularly attend a Christian church.

The Church of England

The Church of England (or the C of E, as it is commonly called) is the official national church of England. Its origins go back to the beginnings of organized Christianity in Britain. Pope Gregory (c. 540–604) sent a monk named Augustine (later to be Saint Augustine) from Rome to Britain to convert the Anglo-Saxons to Christianity. In less than 100 years, the Saxon kingdoms of England were all Christian. In those early times, the English church was a mixture of Roman Catholicism with Celtic and local religious influences and practices. Monasteries were centers of scholarship and the source of the earliest written manuscripts in England. Early Latin translations of the Bible and the earliest Old English manuscripts were written down by English monks in the monasteries. Viking invasions in the ninth century destroyed many monasteries. After the Norman Conquest (1066), the English church was reformed in line with Roman Catholicism.

Break from Rome

The break from Roman Catholicism came during the reign of Henry VIII (1491–1547). Pope Clement VII (1478–1534) refused to grant Henry a divorce from his wife, Catherine of Aragon, so that he could marry Anne Boleyn. Henry forced Parliament to pass a series of acts that separated the English church from Rome. In 1534, by the Act of Supremacy, Henry was named supreme head of the Church of England. The effect of that legislation was to remove the pope as the supreme authority of the Church of England and replace him with the supreme authority of the English Crown, namely the

This frontispiece for the Book of Common Prayer was printed in 1549. The Prayer Book, which is used as the liturgical book for Anglican services, has been revised several times.

king or queen. This was the beginning of the union of church and state in England. Ever since then, the British monarch has been head of the Church of England. Henry also broke up the monasteries, beginning in 1536. He considered the monasteries to be centers of Roman Catholic power in England and therefore an obstacle to his aims to separate the English church from Rome. The devout Catholic queen Mary I (1516–1558) persecuted and repressed Protestants. Her successor, Queen Elizabeth I (1533–1603), confirmed the Church of England's independence and Protestant leanings.

The first Act of Uniformity of 1549 authorized the Book of Common Prayer as the standard work of Church of England liturgy and doctrine. Thomas Cranmer (1489–1556), appointed archbishop of Canterbury by Henry VIII in 1533, prepared the first Book of Common Prayer (or the Prayer Book, as it is commonly called). Cranmer's aim with the Prayer Book was to create a middle ground between Catholic and Protestant doctrines that combined features of both. He wanted to establish a single uniform English-style ("Anglican") liturgy that reflected the Church of England's independence from Rome. The Prayer Book was revised a number of times over the next hundred years to make changes according to religious and political views of the day. The final 1662 version is now the standard liturgy for the Church of England. It is also a basic source of doctrine for the Anglican mother church, the Church of England.

English Bibles

In the sixteenth and seventeenth centuries, the first printed English-language versions of the Bible were published. William Tyndale (c. 1494–1536) believed that

The interior of Salisbury Cathedral has vaulted ceilings. Salisbury Cathedral was built between 1220 and 1258. The cathedral has the tallest spire in England, which stretches 404 feet (123 m) into the sky.

ordinary people should be able to read the Bible in English. Until then, the Bible had only been available in Latin. Tyndale's English-language translation of the New Testament was printed in Cologne, Germany, and was first published in 1525. It became known as Tyndale's Bible. Its language and style became the foundation for later English-language versions of the Bible. The first complete Bible to be printed in the English language was published by Miles Coverdale (1488?–1569) in 1535. The Coverdale Bible was translated into English from German and Latin sources. Coverdale also used Tyndale's translation of the New Testament. The Coverdale Bible was printed in Antwerp, Belgium. The second edition of the Coverdale Bible, published in 1537, is known as Matthew's Bible. It was the first Bible printed in England. The Great Bible (so called because of its large size), also known as Cranmer's Bible, was published in 1539 to 1540. It was the first official version of the Bible for use by Protestants in England. King James I (1603–1625) organized a group of scholars to produce the Authorized Version of the Bible, published in 1611. The Authorized Bible (also called the

King James Bible) is based on the earlier English Bibles, particularly on Tyndale's clear and simple language. The King James Bible (with some later changes) is the standard version used by Protestants around the world today.

Anglicanism

Anglicanism is the blend of Catholicism and Protestantism practiced in the Church of England. The Anglican Communion is the loosely organized family of churches around the world that conforms generally to the Church of England doctrine. The Church of England is the mother church for its local offshoots in other countries, which are known collectively as the Anglican Communion, or Anglican churches worldwide. The Anglican Church generally is quite flexible and practical in its rituals and beliefs. It allows considerable liberty in the way its principles and beliefs are interpreted. In most matters, it allows for a practical rather than strict interpretation of Anglican doctrine.

Church of England Organization

The Church of England itself is organized into two provinces: the southern province, led by the archbishop of Canterbury, and the northern province, led by the archbishop of York. The two archbishops are appointed by the monarch with the advice of the prime minister as head of the church. Canterbury (and its archbishop) is the spiritual head of the Church of England. He is Primate of All England and

The archbishop of Canterbury, Dr. Rowan Williams, was ordained archbishop on February 27, 2003. Williams was born in Wales and was the archbishop of Wales from 1999 to 2002.

ranks above the archbishop of York. In July 2002, Dr. Rowan Williams was elected as the 104th archbishop of Canterbury. (Augustine was the first, in AD 597.)

Under these two provinces are forty-three dioceses. Each diocese is headed by a bishop appointed by the monarch. Dioceses are divided into parishes. There are 13,000 Church of England parishes. The parishes each have a local parish priest. These are more commonly called vicars or rectors. Vicars, together with their bishops, are responsible for the spiritual well-being of everyone living within their parish. Vicars in England often get involved in secular as well as religious parish issues. Unlike Catholic priests who take the vow of celibacy (not having sex), vicars and other officials of the Church of England marry and have families.

Deacons are assistants to Church of England vicars. Women deacons, called deaconesses, were first allowed to become vicars in the Church of England in 1987. They could perform all the functions of a male vicar except for the celebration of the Eucharist (the Holy Communion: the sacrament of the Lord's Supper by which the vicar gives bread and wine to worshipers during the church service). In 1992, the church voted to ordain women as fully fledged priests.

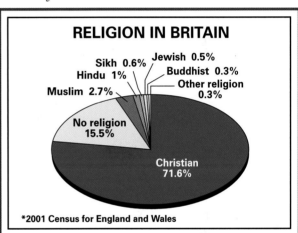

RELIGION IN BRITAIN

Sikh 0.6%
Hindu 1%
Muslim 2.7%
Jewish 0.5%
Buddhist 0.3%
Other religion 0.3%
No religion 15.5%
Christian 71.6%

*2001 Census for England and Wales

Religious Diversity in England

Methodism

Methodism is one of the main offshoots of English Anglicanism. Its founder, John Wesley (1703–1791), was ordained in the Church of England. Around 1738, he founded the Society of Methodists. The main sources of Methodist inspiration are the Bible, traditional Christian principles toward the "perfect love" of God, concern for the underprivileged, and guidance by the Holy Spirit. In 1795, English

Pictured at left is Canterbury Cathedral, one of the oldest Christian structures in England. The cathedral was built and renovated over many hundreds of years, from around the twelfth century to 1950. The archbishop of Canterbury, who is the chief cleric of all of England, leads from Canterbury Cathedral. Above is a graph showing the religions of England. The largest religion practiced in England is Christianity at 71.6 percent.

John Francis Bentley built Westminster Cathedral between 1895 and 1903. It is the most important Catholic church in England.

Methodism split from the Church of England. The new church encouraged its followers to live simple lives and endure economic hardship. In the Victorian period (most of the nineteenth century), Methodism was associated mainly with working-class communities. In England, its strength still lies in traditionally working-class areas in the north of England and in Cornwall in the southwest.

Catholics

There are an estimated 4 million Catholics in England. Around 10 percent of them regularly attend church. Catholics were persecuted in England following Henry VIII's break with Rome. It was not until 1829 that Catholics regained the right to be elected to Parliament. Today, the Catholic Church in England and Wales is divided into five regional provinces made up of twenty-one smaller districts called dioceses. The main diocese of each province is called the archdiocese. The bishop of each archdiocese is an archbishop. The archbishop of Westminster, the Most Reverend Cormac Murphy-O'Connor, became the latest

In March 2000, the archbishop of Westminster, Cormac Murphy-O'Connor, waves to the crowd following a ceremony in which he was declared the head of the Roman Catholic Church of England.

Tony Blair *(second from left)*, meets with leaders of the Muslim community to discuss the Islamic Response to Terrorism Conference.

head of the Catholic Church in England and Wales in March 2000.

Other Religions

The arrival of immigrants from Asia and Africa, especially in the twentieth century, brought many different religions to England. There are now 1.5 million Muslims and more than 300 mosques in Britain. Hindus number about 600,000, and there are around 350,000 Sikhs (followers of the Indian Sikh religion, which combines features of Islam and Hinduism). Edward I (1239–1307) expelled the Jews from Britain in 1290. They returned as immigrants from the seventeenth century onward. The practicing Jewish community in England today is surprisingly small—fewer than 500,000—although there are probably many more than that with Jewish roots. Jewish congregations in Britain make up the second-largest Jewish community in Europe.

Dr. Jonathan Sacks, England's chief rabbi, speaks during an interview in 2002. Sacks has been the chief rabbi since 1991, and has started several projects to benefit the Jewish community in England.

THE ART AND ARCHITECTURE OF ENGLAND

7

T he early Christian church first nurtured the visual arts (painting, sculpture, and architecture) in England. Monks working in monasteries took years to complete single hand-painted illuminated manuscripts. These were usually sacred texts from the Gospels, made in the centuries before the invention of the printing press in the fifteenth century. The most famous illuminated manuscripts are the Lindisfarne Gospels, which are now in the British Museum, in London.

Painting

The eighteenth and nineteenth centuries' three greatest English painters—J. M. W. Turner (1775–1851), John Constable (1776–1837), and Thomas Gainsborough (1727–1788)—were masters of landscape and portrait painting. The most original (and controversial) English painter of the twentieth century was Francis Bacon (1909–1992). The figures in his works are almost always contorted, often grotesquely so. In the late twentieth century, Britain became a world center for so-called BritArt, imaginative new styles of art that challenge our perceptions of what art is.

Thomas Gainsborough was born in the Suffolk countryside. He studied painting in London and lived at various times in London, Suffolk, and the elegant country town of Bath in western England. Gainsborough has been called the most versatile

Pictured at left is architect Richard Roger's Lloyd's of London building. Rogers was born in Florence, Italy, and became a British citizen. He is noted for his modernist style. Above is J. M. W. Turner's watercolor of Caernarfon Castle, which the English landscape artist painted around 1832.

Thomas Gainsborough painted *Miss Lloyd* in 1750. The painting shows a girl from Ipswitch sitting in a park.

English painter of the eighteenth century. He was the only one to paint both portraits and landscapes in equal measure. He declared early in his life that he preferred to paint landscapes. Portraits, however, earned more money, since they were often commissioned by the subject or subjects.

John Constable is the most English of all English painters. His landscapes, especially of the Suffolk and Essex countryside near his birthplace, are precise and realistic expressions of rural England in the nineteenth century. Constable was born in the small village of East Burgholt, on the Suffolk-Essex border, northeast of London. Constable painted mainly those landscapes he remembered as a child: village lanes, the fields and meadows around the river Stour, barges drawn by horses down the canal, and the canal locks at Dedham and Flatford. By the time he married in 1816, at the age of forty, he had painted some of his most famous early works: *Boatbuilding near Flatford Mill*, *The Stour Valley and Dedham Village*, and *Dedham Vale: Morning*. He sketched and painted in the open air to record the form, colors, atmosphere, and light of the landscape. These sketches are considered among Constable's most important achievements for their individuality and uniqueness. *The Hay-Wain*, first exhibited in

English artist John Constable painted *Cottage in a Cornfield* in 1833. Dedham Vale, where he made many of his works, is now known as Constable County.

Head VI was painted by artist Francis Bacon in 1949. Bacon was influenced by Diego Velázquez and Pablo Picasso. He also admired the filmmaker Luis Buñuel.

1821, is Constable's most famous of his larger formal paintings. After Constable's death in 1837, his reputation increased. In 1843, his first biographer, C. R. Leslie, wrote that Constable was "the most genuine painter of English landscape." That opinion still holds true to this day.

Francis Bacon was born in 1909 in Dublin, Ireland, of English parents. He left home at the age of sixteen and became a self-taught artist after settling in London in 1928. *Three Studies for Figures at the Base of a Crucifixion* (1944) first established Bacon as a major artist of an original, if controversial, style. All of Bacon's works show figures in tortured, twisted poses that almost shriek with the thrill of exposing the harsh reality of life. In many of his paintings, Bacon used the images of photographs and subjects of other painters (such as the great Spanish artist Diego Velázquez) and re-created them as distorted figures of his own expression. He was homosexual and lived a rather wild, bohemian life among other artists in the Soho district of London. He died in Madrid, Spain, in 1992.

Sculpture

The earliest examples of English sculpture were the carved Christian and Celtic stone crosses of Anglo-Saxon times. Stone carving reached a high point in the elaborate stonework of English cathedrals and abbeys in the Gothic style of the Middle Ages. Over the following centuries, sculpture in England was mainly in the form of public monuments. It was not until the twentieth century that a truly personal style of original sculpture emerged in England.

Henry Moore (1898–1986) was born into a working-class family in a small coal-mining town near Leeds, in the north of England. After World War I (1914–1917), he

Sculptor Henry Moore cast *Reclining Figure* in bronze between 1969 and 1970. Besides reclining figures, Moore used the theme of a mother and child in many of his sculptures.

studied sculpture at the Leeds School of Art, where he met the other great English sculptor of the twentieth century, Barbara Hepworth (1903–1975). Early in his career, Moore was strongly influenced by the Mayan sculptural style of Mexico and in particular the stylized, chunky figures of Mayan spirits. Moore's work became increasingly abstract, based loosely but not exclusively on the reclining human figure. His aim was to express the rhythms and forms of nature in his sculpture. Today, his massive sculptures in wood, stone, marble, and bronze are prized works of modern art in collections around the world.

Dame Barbara Hepworth was born near Henry Moore in Wakefield. At the age of fifteen, she decided to become a sculptor. Her work became even more abstract in form than Moore's, especially under the influence of her second husband, the English abstract painter Ben Nicholson. In the late 1930s and 1940s, she focused on the relationship in her sculptures between the mass of the work and the empty spaces surrounding and within it. She died in 1975 in a fire at her home in St. Ives, Cornwall. The house is now a museum housing many of her works.

Architecture

English architecture dates back 4,000 years to the Iron Age settlements of southern England, neolithic burial chambers, and, the most famous pre-Christian structure of all, Stonehenge. A few examples of Anglo-Saxon churches from the eighth and ninth centuries have survived. Otherwise, the earliest English buildings still used to this day date from just before the time of the Norman Conquest. For the most part, English architecture as we know it today started with the Normans, almost 1,000 years ago.

Thatched Cottages, Country Manors, and Cathedral Spires

The architectural landscape of England is dotted with churches and cathedrals, manor houses and palaces, and thatched-roof cottages. The first great cathedrals of England were constructed just after the Norman Conquest. The four greatest early English cathedrals—Canterbury, Wells, Lincoln, and Salisbury—were built in the Gothic Norman style of the eleventh to the thirteenth centuries. The foundations of Westminster Abbey, in Central London, were laid from 1045 to 1050 but were rebuilt after 1066. Durham Cathedral, built over the period from 1093 to 1133, is considered to be the finest Norman building in England. Some smaller parish churches from the Norman period also survive. One of the finest examples is at Iffley, near Oxford, constructed between 1170 and 1180. Malmesbury Abbey (1160–1170), in Wiltshire, has a beautiful example of the elaborately carved stone doorways typical of Norman church decoration.

All around England, there are hundreds of large country mansions and palaces. These were first built around the time of Henry VIII. Henry's royal palace at Hampton Court, just outside London, was one of the first and finest examples. These mansions and palaces were all built to reflect the stature and greatness of their owners. The greatest private residence in England is Buckingham Palace, the official London residence of the queen. George III (1738–1820) bought Buckingham House for his wife, Queen Charlotte, to use as a family home. In 1820, George IV (1762–1830) employed John Nash (1752–1835), the most famous English architect of the day, to transform the house

Buckingham Palace is one of England's most famous landmarks. The road that leads to the palace is called the Mall. The gardens at the palace are often the setting for Queen Elizabeth II's summer tea parties.

Devon is known for its cottages with thatched roofs, such as the one seen here, and its rolling hillsides. The north of Devon is provincial and has very few major towns. Many Britons come to Devon for vacations because of its peaceful, rural setting.

into a royal palace. Queen Victoria was the first British sovereign to live in Buckingham Palace. In the twentieth century, the palace was the scene of historic public appearances by the royal family.

Thatched cottages are a traditional English style of architecture. Most are at least a few hundred years old. The roofs of these houses are made with bundles of dried water reeds (thatch). These are tied together and attached to the beams of the roof. The thatch makes a waterproof covering and must be replaced every twenty years or so.

Great English Architects

The first prominent English architect was Inigo Jones (1573–1652). He brought to England the Italian Renaissance concepts of architectural harmony and proportion. Jones built mainly grand, palatial buildings, only a few of which survive. Two of the most prominent are in London: the Banqueting House (originally part of Whitehall Palace and now a government building) and the Protestant Church of St. Paul, in

This seaside hotel and restaurant are located in Kent. Kent is a scenic county and is nicknamed the Garden of England. There are many hop farms (for making beer) and orchards throughout Kent.

Covent Garden. From 1633 to 1642, Jones undertook restoration work on Old St. Paul's Cathedral. His work on St. Paul's influenced his most famous successor, Sir Christopher Wren (1632–1723), the greatest of all English architects. The Great Fire of London in 1666 destroyed or damaged Old St. Paul's Cathedral, eighty-seven parish churches, and more than 13,000 houses. Afterward, Wren was commissioned to rebuild many churches, public buildings, and most notably, St. Paul's Cathedral. The dome of St. Paul's Cathedral is today the most famous architectural monument to the greatness of Sir Christopher Wren.

Lancelot "Capability" Brown (1715–1783) was England's greatest landscape architect. He began life as a gardener's assistant. In the early 1750s, he began designing gardens on his own. Within a few years, he became the foremost garden designer in the country. His great talent was to create harmonious natural landscapes within the grounds of private country estates.

The Tower Bridge of London crosses the Thames River. The Tower Bridge, built from 1886 to 1894, was recently opened to pedestrians. Along the walkway there is an exhibit about the bridge's history.

THE LITERATURE AND MUSIC OF ENGLAND

8

L iterature, rather than the visual arts (painting and sculpture) or music, is the best-known feature of English artistic culture. English writers are read and appreciated by millions—probably billions—of people around the world. No other country has as many writers who are read so widely. For his contribution to world literature, William Shakespeare is considered one of the greatest Englishmen who ever lived. England has produced some great classical composers, but they are few in number compared with its writers. Today, English theater and drama, especially in London, is among the best in the world.

Literature

The first literature in England was Anglo-Saxon poetry from around the eighth century. Today, we need to translate those early poems into Modern English to understand them. Geoffrey Chaucer (c. 1342–1400) is usually considered to be the first writer of Modern English literature. The greatest (but not the first) English drama

(plays) appeared in the late 1500s and 1600s. William Shakespeare (1564–1616) stood head and shoulders above all others. Ben Jonson (1572–1637) and Christopher Marlowe (1564–1593) were the two other leading playwrights of that time. The first English novels were written in the seventeenth century.

Pictured at left, two dancers perform in Sergei Prokofiev's ballet *Romeo and Juliet*. The Shakespeare play is one of the most famous stories in the world. It has been adapted into ballets, films, books, and operas. Pictured above, Shakespearean actors perform *The Merchant of Venice* in traditional costumes at the Globe Theatre. The Globe was one of four major theaters in England during Shakespeare's day. The others were the Swan, the Hope, and the Rose.

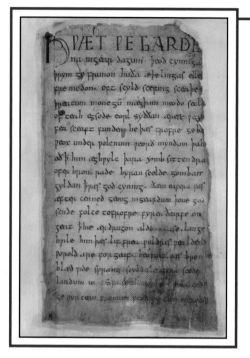

This is the opening manuscript page of the epic poem *Beowulf*. It is from a fifteenth-century manuscript and is written in Old English.

Beowulf

When the Angles came to England in the sixth century, they brought the story of Beowulf with them. The poem we know today as *Beowulf* was composed between 700 and 750 and first written down around 1000. Written in Old English, it is the earliest epic poem of English literature. The story begins with the monster Grendel, who is attacking the king of the Danes, Hrothgar. A young warrior, Beowulf, comes to Hrothgar's rescue. He kills Grendel and, later, Grendel's mother, a monster at the bottom of a lake.

The second part of the story is about Beowulf as a king and as an old man who has to defend his kingdom from a fiery dragon. Beowulf kills the dragon but is mortally wounded. The poem ends with the death and funeral of the heroic Beowulf. The poem combines pre-Christian pagan ethics of heroism, courage, and destiny with the values of the new Christian spirit, especially the struggle of good against evil.

Chaucer

Geoffrey Chaucer was the first modern poet of the English language. His most famous work is *The Canterbury Tales*. Written in Middle English, *The Canterbury Tales* has been translated many

This page is part of "The Knight's Tale," from *The Canterbury Tales*, written by Geoffrey Chaucer.

times into modern English, as well as into many other languages. The subject of *The Canterbury Tales* is a pilgrimage (a religious journey) by about thirty pilgrims who are traveling from the Tabard Inn in Southwark, south London, to the shrine of Thomas Becket at Canterbury Cathedral. In the general prologue (the introduction), Chaucer describes each of the pilgrims. They include people from all walks of medieval life. The host at the inn suggests that each pilgrim tell two stories on the way to Canterbury and two on the way back, as entertainment during the journey. The host promises a free dinner to whoever tells the best story. Only twenty-three pilgrims actually tell stories (Chaucer himself, as the narrator, tells two). And there is no return journey. *The Canterbury Tales* is still read today because of its humor and humanity, its vivid expression of life in medieval England, and, not least, because its stories are so entertaining.

Shakespeare

The greatest playwright and greatest of all English literary figures is William Shakespeare. Shakespeare was born in the western England town of Stratford-upon-Avon. Around 1585, he went to London to be an actor. In 1599, Shakespeare and other actors got together to build the Globe Theater. (The Globe was reconstructed in the 1990s to stage plays by Shakespeare and other Elizabethan [in the time of Queen Elizabeth I] playwrights). Shakespeare wrote poetry as well as thirty-seven plays. Up until the middle of the eighteenth century, his poems and especially his sonnets (fourteen-line poems) were more popular

This title page from William Shakespeare's *Comedies, Histories, and Tragedies* includes Shakespeare's portrait. Martin Droeshout engraved this page in 1623.

Stratford-upon-Avon is the birthplace of William Shakespeare. Today, Stratford is home to the Royal Shakespeare Company and the Royal Shakespeare Theatre. Stratford has also preserved the homes of Shakespeare's mother and wife.

than his plays. Nowadays, Shakespeare's plays are staged every day all over the world. Ben Jonson, another great English dramatist of the time, wrote of Shakespeare, after his death, "He was not of an age, but for all time!" And so he remains to this day

Milton

John Milton (1608–1674) composed *Paradise Lost* between 1658 and 1663. The work is composed in twelve books. The first lines of Book I summarize the story. It tells "Of Man's first disobedience, and the fruit/Of that forbidden tree, whose mortal taste/Brought death into the world, and all our woe,/With loss of Eden." The poem is "the greatest single (literary) achievement of the seventeenth century," according to Professor John Vickers's assessment of seventeenth-century English literature in *The Oxford Illustrated History of English Literature.* It remains a masterpiece of English epic poetry.

The Romantic Poets

In the first years of the nineteenth century, a group of poets emerged to become the romantic poets of English literature. These poets were William Wordsworth (1770–1850), Samuel Taylor Coleridge (1772–1834), Lord Byron (1788–1824), Percy Bysshe Shelley (1792–1822), and John Keats (1795–1821). They all had a spiritual love of nature and an almost religious interest in their own personal experience, surrounded by the grim realities of industrialization.

The poet John Milton also wrote several puritanical tracts and essays. He wrote about divorce, censorship, and education and usually attacked medieval Catholicism in his writings.

Their poetry reflects the wonders of nature and the self but leads the poet often to spiritual solitude.

The Novel

The first great English novelist was John Bunyan (1628–1688). His greatest work was *The Pilgrim's Progress,* a classic allegory (story whose characters are symbols for individuals or society as a whole) of the journey of life. *Robinson Crusoe,* written by Daniel Defoe (1660–1731) at the age of sixty, was the first English novel that has remained popular to the present day. Other pioneering English novelists were Samuel Richardson (1689–1761), with *Pamela* and *Clarissa*; Henry Fielding (1707–1754), with *Joseph Andrews* and *Tom Jones;* and Laurence Sterne (1713–1768), with *Tristram Shandy.* Later, Jane Austen (1775–1817) wrote novels that are still popular today. *Pride and Prejudice* is her best-known work.

Many people think Charles Dickens (1812–1870) was England's greatest novelist. *The Pickwick Papers* is a masterpiece of comedy. *Oliver Twist* has been reproduced many times on television, film, and stage. Dickens's novels are entertaining. They also sharply criticize the harsh social conditions of life in Victorian England. English literature

Young dancers perform the Morris dance in a town square. Morris is an English folk dance that dates back to 1477. There are numerous types of Morris dance, including Cotswold Morris, North West Morris, and Border Morris.

is full of novelists from the nineteenth century who are still best-sellers today: William Thackeray's (1811–1863) *Vanity Fair*, Emily Brontë's (1818–1848) *Wuthering Heights*, Charlotte Brontë's (1816–1855) *Jane Eyre*, George Eliot's (1819–1880) *Silas Marner* and *Middlemarch*, Thomas Hardy's (1840–1928) *Tess of the D'Urbervilles*, and Robert Louis Stevenson's (1850–1894) *Treasure Island* are among the best known.

Music

English music started with what is called plainsong or Gregorian chant. These were Catholic church melodies of the sixth and seventh centuries, sung by monks in their monasteries. The first notable English composer was William Byrd (1543–1623), around the time of Shakespeare. Byrd was an organist and devout Catholic best known for his sacred music and the development of the English madrigal (a song).

Although there are no English composers of classical music of the stature of Beethoven or Mozart, half a dozen are world class. Henry Purcell (c. 1659–1695) composed music for the church, the royal court, the stage, and for private entertainment. He was one of Europe's most original composers in his lifetime. George Frideric Handel (1685–1759) was born in Germany. After 1710, he spent the rest of his life in England. He became a British citizen in 1726. He composed his greatest work, *The Messiah*, in 1741. Handel died in 1759. He was buried in Poet's Corner in Westminster Abbey, where the greatest English literary figures are laid to rest.

Sir William Gilbert (1836–1911) and Sir Arthur Sullivan (1842–1900) composed comic operas together as Gilbert and Sullivan. Their distinctively English operettas (little operas) include *The Pirates of Penzance* and *The Mikado*. Sir Edward Elgar (1857–1934) was the first internationally renowned English composer since the time of Henry Purcell, 200 years before. Gustav Holst (1874–1934), was a teacher, musician, and internationally renowned composer of English classical music. Ralph Vaughan Williams (1872–1958) combined his study of English folk songs and fifteenth-century English music to compose most of the English classical music of the early twentieth century. Two other famous English composers of classical music in the twentieth century were Sir William Walton (1902–1983) and Sir Benjamin Britten (1913–1976).

Theater and Dance

Theater in England started with traveling troubadours and minstrels playing to village audiences in medieval times. It is now the performing art for which England is best known. The Royal Shakespeare Company (RSC) was founded in 1864 to stage Shakespeare's plays. To this day, it continues to put on plays by Shakespeare and other playwrights of his time.

Dance is at least as old as theater in England. The earliest English folk dancing originated in the fourteenth century. A typically English folk dance style, Morris dancing, is still practiced at local festivals all around England. Ballet and, later, modern dance became established in England, but particularly in London, with the foundation of the Vic-Wells Ballet (now the Royal Ballet) and the Ballet Club (now Dance Rambert) early in the twentieth century. The most famous classical English ballerina of the twentieth century was Dame Margot Fonteyn (1919–1991).

This is an aerial view of the new Globe Theater. The Puritans closed the old Globe Theatre in 1642. It was eventually torn down in 1644 to make room for new tenement houses. The new Globe Theatre reopened in 1997.

FAMOUS FOODS AND RECIPES OF ENGLAND

9

When the Romans first came to England in the first century AD, they found a Celtic people there who lived and ate like primitives. The Celts spent most of their time either fighting, or producing and hunting food. The Romans thought they were savages but soon introduced kitchens, tableware, and decorations to make life more pleasurable. Emperor Agricola, on his arrival in Britain in AD 77, found "a fierce and savage people running wild in the woods." The Romans were capable of eating huge quantities. It was said that one Roman governor of Britain, Clodius Albinus, "could swallow of a morning five hundred figs, a hundred peaches, ten melons, twenty pounds of grapes, a hundred figpeckers [a kind of bird] and four hundred oysters."

The Anglo-Saxons who came after the Romans ate horsemeat. The Christians, however, forbade it, so they could be seen to be different from the un-Christian Anglo-Saxons. To this day, the English have a natural distaste for horsemeat. Anglo-Saxon cooking was otherwise considered to be of excellent quality. There was plenty of food available in the forests, from the rivers, and on the hillsides of Anglo-Saxon England. Meat was not commonly eaten. Cattle were used mainly for plowing the fields. Cows were reared for milk. Farming was very basic, but with a population of less than 2

Pictured at left, an Indian restaurateur in Newcastle happily offers Indian treats to British soldiers who served in Iraq. Pictured above, a woman does her grocery shopping at Tesco, England's largest supermarket chain.

Edith Mary Garner (1881–1955) painted this picture of the Romford Market.

million, there was plenty of land for everyone. Ale and wine, brewed in the home, were the most common drinks.

Food in Medieval England

In medieval times, rich people ate huge amounts of food. Their one main meal of the day was a feast of roasted meats, stews, soups, and sauces. Spices other than salt were not common until around the thirteenth century. Then, soldiers returning to England from the Crusades in the Middle East brought with them ginger, cloves, nutmeg, cinnamon, and many other spices not known in England until this time. Spices were only for the rich. Poor peasants (meaning, most people) used salt but not much else to flavor their food.

For the peasants, of course, life was not quite so wonderful. They caught what they could from the countryside, made coarse bread from wheat bran, and generally lived on a diet of wheat and barley porridge (hot cooked cereal), eggs, and peas and beans. The only meat they ate was from wild birds (such as partridge) they caught in the fields. Most people ate what was available locally and according to the season. Winter for most people was a big problem. If the harvest was poor and they could not store enough food to last the winter, people went hungry. Ale helped ease the hardships of medieval life: It was drunk by everyone as "a universal occupation," according to William of Malemesbury (circa 1090–1143). It was recorded that the nuns of Syon Abbey each got a ration of seven gallons (twenty-seven liters) of ale a week. Wine was also common. Water was often of very bad quality and considered a poor man's drink.

A painting by Joseph Nash depicts a banquet in the baronial hall of Penshurst Place, 1838. Penshurst Place is one of the oldest family homes in England. It was built during the thirteenth century.

The Elizabethans

In the Elizabethan age, explorers brought new foods to England from around the world: tea from India and China to replace ale and wine, chocolate and potatoes from Mexico and South America, coffee from the Middle East, and sugar from the Caribbean. The Protestant Puritans of the sixteenth century disliked too much pleasure, so Christmas feasting diminished. So did the consumption of alcohol and even the excessive use of spices. English food from then on would be plainer than it had been before. It was from this time, too, that a dislike of foreigners began. European Catholics were the enemy of Protestant England. "Catholic" came to mean "foreigner" to the Elizabethan mind. And that included foreign food. By the seventeenth century, "There was a middle class hostility [in England] towards foreigners and foreign things, especially towards foreign food," according to food historian Philippa Pullar.

England was becoming a nation of meat eaters. Roast beef was the favorite. As the poet Richard Leveridge wrote in 1735:

> When Mighty Roast Beef was the Englishman's Food,
> It ennobled our veins and enriched our Blood,
> Our Soldiers were brave, and our Courtiers were good,
> On the Roast Beef of Old England,
> And Old English Roast Beef!

Tea replaced beer as the national drink in the seventeenth and eighteenth centuries. It was drunk without milk, which was considered unhealthy for human consumption. At the time, milk was sold straight from the cow, in dirty buckets, and often watered down.

The Food Revolution

The Industrial Revolution of seventeenth- and eighteenth-century England brought with it a food revolution. The population of England rose dramatically. Between 1066 and 1800, the population increased only from 2 million to 9 million. In the next fifty years, by 1850, it had doubled to 18 million. In the next sixty years, it doubled again to 36 million. From the mid-1700s, there was a huge migration of people away from the countryside. They went to the towns and cities to work in factories. Food had to be transported to them from the countryside. For the first time in England's history, food was transported long distances, away from where it was produced to where it was consumed. The quality of fresh food declined during its transport. Apart from that, food was commonly changed by adding dangerous substances to add weight so that it would sell for more money. The situation became so bad that, in 1872, the government passed the Adulteration of Food, Drink and Drugs Act. The act prohibited the addition of any substance to food for the purpose of adding weight.

Many people got rich during the Industrial Revolution. Even more people became very much poorer. The factory and mill workers earned wages that kept them in poverty. Their diet was often bread and jam and scraps of leftover vegetables. Their health declined. A famous journalist and politician of the early 1800s, William Cobbett (1763–1835), wrote about how the Industrial Revolution was destroying the life of "rural England." "Nowadays," he wrote, "all is looked for at shops. To buy the thing [food] ready made is the taste of the day: thousands who are housekeepers buy their dinners ready cooked." Most people before the Industrial Revolution ate their food where they grew it: in the countryside. After the start of the Industrial Revolution, food came to be produced more and more by the few people left in the countryside for the many more people living in towns and cities.

By the time of World War I (1914–1918), the health of most people in England was poor because of poor-quality food. Even after the war, meat was seldom eaten more than once a week. Fresh milk was rare. In 1931, the government set up an advisory committee on nutrition. The aim was to provide decent-quality food at prices the public could afford. In 1939, when World War II began, the government brought in ration books. Each person exchanged a coupon from their ration books for a certain amount of meat, sugar, fat, and so on every week. Amounts were frugal, but for many people it was the first balanced diet they had ever had. Rationing ended in 1953. Cheap food became abundant for everyone.

The full English breakfast is a royal morning feast. Many cafés and hotels in England serve breakfast all day long.

The New Food Culture

Nowadays, food in England is even more abundant. It is varied, relatively cheap (compared to people's incomes), and relatively healthy (regulated by the Food Standards Agency). The big supermarket chains sell 75 percent of all the food British people buy. Buying from supermarkets is convenient, but it has meant that thousands of traditional kinds of food stores (fishmongers, greengrocers, and butchers) have gone out of business.

Since the 1980s, dozens of new kinds of food have become available in England (and all Britain). The most popular food to take away (to get to go) used to be fish and chips. Now the most popular takeaway dish in England is chicken tikka masala, made by thousands of Indian restaurants around the country. The demand for different styles of food has since expanded. People are constantly looking for something new. There are dozens of television programs about food and cooking, and there are as many celebrity chefs. Hundreds of new cookbooks are published every year. And yet, for all the variety available, the British still seem to like their own food best. A 2003 survey found that the favorite dish in Britain was the great English breakfast! This consists of fried eggs, sausages, bacon, fried tomatoes, fried bread (slices of bread deep-fried in oil), baked beans, and a cup of tea. Extras might include fried kidneys or "black pudding" (a thick sausage made from pork blood and fat), barley, and oatmeal. Other favorite British foods include roast beef and Yorkshire pudding; fish and chips; cream tea (scones, which are like muffins, spread with jam and thick cream to have with tea); custard with any sweet dessert; kippers (herrings split in two and smoke-cured); and meat pies (especially pork pies).

Cookbooks and Mrs. Beeton

The first cookbooks in England were simply notes showing what ingredients to use to make certain dishes: a handful of this, a pinch of that. There were no measurements or cooking times and temperatures. Just cook till it's done! One of the first

Roast Beef and Yorkshire Pudding

Roast Beef

Preheat the oven to 550°F (290°C). Take a 4- to 5-pound (1.8- to 2.3-kilogram) rib or sirloin of beef and season it all over with salt and pepper. Place it fat side up on a rack in a roasting pan, then put it in the oven. Reduce the heat immediately to 350°F (180°C). Cook the meat for 20 minutes per pound (25 minutes per kg) plus 20 minutes for rare; 25 minutes per pound (35 minutes per kg) plus 25 minutes for medium; and 30 minutes per pound (40 minutes per kg) plus 30 minutes for well done. As the meat cooks, baste it every 15 to 20 minutes with its cooking juices. When the meat is done, take it out of the oven and put it on a platter. Set the beef aside for about 20 minutes to rest. (This gives time for the meat and juices inside it to relax and settle, giving it better flavor.)

Yorkshire Pudding

The most important thing to remember about making Yorkshire pudding is that you must pour the batter into very hot fat in the baking tin. The hot fat from the roast beef will give the best flavor. Use a metal baking tin (or muffin tray); ovenproof glass or ceramic baking dishes make the pudding soggy.

¼ C. white flour	7 ounces (200 ml) milk
Pinch of salt	3 ounces (100 ml) water
1 large egg	

Mix the flour and salt in a bowl. Break the egg into the center of the flour. Add half the milk. Mix with the flour and egg. Beat until smooth. Add the rest of the milk and the water. Beat until smooth. Leave the batter to rest. As soon as the beef comes out of the oven, spoon a little hot fat from the roasting pan into a muffin tin with twelve cups, about 1/4 inch (0.6 centimeters) in each cup. Put the muffin tin in the oven to get the fat as hot as possible. Take it out after five minutes. Pour the batter into each muffin cup, filling them to about three-quarters full. Bake at 425°F (220°C) for 15 to 20 minutes until risen and golden brown (while the beef is resting). Do not open the oven door while the puddings are cooking. Remove when done and serve with the roast beef.

Delia Smith, a TV chef and cookbook writer, signs copies of one of her books in 1995. She has led English cooks away from such foods as roast beef and cooked cabbage to roasted tomato risotto and other Italian dishes.

British cookbooks was *The Form of Cury,* from the twelfth century ("cury" is an old word for cooked food). Many of the 196 "recipes" in it were of French origin, probably because the Normans (from France) had invaded England just a hundred years before, in 1066. The invention of the printing press in the fifteenth century and the later growth of the middle classes brought more books available to more readers. There were also more big family homes after the sixteenth century. Cookbooks from the seventeenth century included not only recipes but also advice on how to manage the household. *Mrs. Beeton's Cookery and Household Management* was written by Isabella Beeton (1836–1865) and published around 1860. Mrs. Beeton's book of more than 1,000 pages included all kinds of advice for keeping a household in Victorian England, along with a collection of food recipes.

Elizabeth David: The Awakening of Taste

Just after World War II, a young Englishwoman by the name of Elizabeth David (1914–1992) published *A Book of Mediterranean Food.* It was the first in a series of books she wrote about the cooking of France and Italy. Her cookbooks opened the eyes and aroused the appetites of English people who had been used to plain and rather boring English food all their lives. Her experiences of the vibrant, simple, and fresh foods of the Mediterranean, contrasted with English food, inspired her to write about them. Her books awakened English people to the possibility of new tastes and styles of food, cooking, and eating. She later went on to write about traditional English food. After her came a flood of cookbooks about every food subject under the sun. Elizabeth David, however, was the pioneer.

DAILY LIFE AND CUSTOMS IN ENGLAND

Quite a lot of family life in England today revolves around some form of information technology (IT): computers, the Internet, e-mail, mobile phones, and so on. A lot of time is spent in front of a monitor attached either to a computer or the television. (The British watch more television, on average, than any other nationality in Europe.) Computer games and text messaging (sending short messages by mobile phone to other mobile phone users) are extremely popular.

A generation ago, few people in England had enough money to spend on the kinds of IT equipment we take for granted today. A car was a luxury in 1960. Today, half of all households in Britain own a car (and 30 percent have two). In 1970, a good annual income was £7,000 ($12,000). The average income in England today is about £20,000 ($32,000) per year. In the 1980s and 1990s, people were encouraged to buy their own homes, instead of renting. Two-thirds of the adult UK population now own their own homes.

There are now many more single people living on their own, or with a partner, than a generation ago. The traditional family of two parents and a few children is still the most common kind of English family, but there are more nontraditional households than in the past. Divorce, for example, has become much more common: in 2002,

Pictured at left, spectators at the Ascot Races sport classic hats. In keeping with the wealthy traditions of the race, men wear coattails and top hats. The women wear the latest fashions. Pictured above is the Hampton Court Maze at Hampton Court Palace. The maze was grown in 1690 during the reign of William III. It covers a third of an acre and has over 0.5 miles (0.8 km) of paths.

The 2001 census revealed these facts about the structure of family life in Britain today:

- Almost one-third of all families have children.
- Eleven percent of unmarried couples have children.
- Eight percent of homes are rented.
- The average size of households (families) in England is 2.36 individuals (and getting smaller).
- Sixty-five percent of the 11.7 million children (younger than sixteen) in England and Wales live with their natural parents, 23 percent live in a single-parent household, and 10 percent live in a stepfamily (where one or both of the parents have remarried).

Marital Status of English and Welsh Population

Remarried 7.1%
Separated 2.5%
Divorced 8.0%
Widowed 8.4%
Married 43.8%
Single 30.2%

Source: 2001 Census for England and Wales

there were 160,000 divorces in Britain compared with just 27,000 in 1961. Around 8 percent of the population is divorced. This has created many households with a single parent and children. The 2001 census revealed that "almost one in four children in England and Wales now lives in a one-parent family."

Britain is still a mainly white, Christian society. In the 2001 Census for England and Wales, 91.3 percent of people described themselves as white, 4.4 percent said they were Asian (Indian, Pakistani, Bangladeshi, or other), and 2.2 percent described themselves as black (from the Caribbean, Africa, or elsewhere). Just more than 1 percent described themselves as "mixed race." More than 70 percent of English and Welsh people said they were Christians, 3 percent were Muslims, and 1 percent were Hindu. Only 0.5 percent said they were Jewish. Muslims have become the second-largest religious group in Britain, with about 1.5 million people. Muslim communities are concentrated in cities such as London, Bradford, and Leicester, where the first immigrants settled.

Leisure, Recreation, and Sports

In most towns in England, there is a public leisure center, with a swimming pool, gym, fitness center, and spa. Private health clubs and fitness centers are one of the fastest-growing businesses in Britain today. Pubs are still a focal point of English

This well-groomed forest is located at the center of the Royal Horticulture Society (RHS) in Surrey. The RHS was founded 200 years ago. It is the largest gardening organization in the world.

life, to meet friends, and have a few pints (of beer) or a meal. Wine bars were the first competitors to the pub, in the 1970s. Their popularity has since declined. American- and European-style coffee bars have since sprouted up everywhere. Eating out is almost as popular as going to the pub. Indian restaurants are the most popular, for their low prices and good value. Thai, Chinese, Spanish, French, Italian, and Middle Eastern restaurants have become part of the English landscape. Although there are very few restaurants specializing in English or British food, the old-fashioned local "chippy" (a restaurant that serves fish and chips [french fries]) is still going strong.

To get away from the hustle and bustle of town and city life, many people head for the nearest bit of countryside to enjoy the greenery, walk along public footpaths, and stretch their legs. Walking and cycling through the countryside are probably the most common outdoors activities in Britain. Parts of the countryside are protected as Areas of Outstanding Natural Beauty. There are dozens of big country houses with landscaped gardens open to the public. Gardening is another traditional leisure activity. There are gardening programs on television (hosted by their own celebrity gardeners!), international garden exhibitions, and gardening books in the hundreds.

Holidays

A two-week vacation for most English people used to mean staying at a little boardinghouse or guesthouse by the English seaside. Traditional English seaside resorts such as Margate and Brighton on the south coast and Blackpool in Lancashire have since declined. More people now go abroad on "package holidays" (flight and hotel

Vacationers wade in the waters at Blackpool Beach in Lancashire. Blackpool has an amusement park, several nightclubs, and restaurants, and hosts arts and entertainment festivals in the summer.

packaged together at a cheap price). The first package holidays came out in the 1960s. Spain and Greece became the most popular destinations because they had sun and cheap food and wine. Since then people have spread their wings to holiday in Thailand, the Caribbean, and thousands of other destinations in every corner of the globe. Spain is still the biggest foreign tourist destination for the British; around 14 million British visitors went to Spain in 2002. Quite a few people still take vacations in England, of course. Cornwall and Devon in the southwest are summer favorites. The Peak District and Lake District in the north are popular for hikers. Many people rent a cottage in the countryside or on the coast for two weeks.

Sports

Cricket is the English sport. The amateur game is played on weekends on pitches (grounds) all around England. The professional game is played throughout the summer

(mid-April to early September) by teams representing English counties. Nothing is more typical of an English summer scene than a cricket

English slip fielder Mark Butcher plays cricket at Lord's Cricket Ground. Lord's Cricket Ground is a playing field in Saint John's Wood in London. Many refer to it as the Home of Cricket.

match being played by two teams in their all-white uniforms. A scattering of spectators usually lounges in front of the clubhouse, offering an occasional murmur of applause for a good shot. The so-called test matches are played between national teams from test match–playing countries; the main ones are England, Australia, New Zealand, India, Pakistan, the West Indies, and South Africa. Two countries play a series of usually three or five test matches. Each match can last up to five days but often finishes before that.

Football (soccer) is England's other national game. A typical winter weekend sight is a playing field with several matches going on, accompanied by the loud support of each team's fans (usually friends and family). The professional leagues play once a week, from mid-August to the following May. There are hundreds of local amateur leagues around the country. The top professional teams (Manchester United, Arsenal, and so on) play in the Premiership League. Below them are four leagues, from the First to the Fourth Division. Attendance at the big professional league matches is like that of baseball, with stadiums holding between 25,000 and 60,000 spectators. There are various national competitions for the professional leagues, but the most prestigious is the Football Association Cup (known as the FA Cup). The ultimate goal of any of the big league teams is to lead the Premiership at the end of the season, win the FA Cup, and win the most prestigious competitions against all the big European clubs. The other great winter sport is rugby. Like football, there are numerous rugby clubs around the country. The biggest international matches are played between England, Scotland, Wales, Ireland, Australia, New Zealand, and South Africa.

Another very typical English game is bowls, played on a well-maintained bowling green (lawn) by players dressed all in white. The game is similar to the French game of *boules*.

An intense soccer match between Mauricio Taricco from the Hotspur team and David Beckham from Manchester United. Beckham is known for his crossing and long, free-range kicks.

This aerial view shows Wimbledon Stadium, where the famous tennis championship is held. At Wimbledon, the Duchess of Kent presents the Champion Cup and Bowl to the winners in a very traditional ceremony.

Tennis was invented in England. The Wimbledon championship (so named because it is held in the London suburb of Wimbledon) is considered the most important tournament in the tennis world. In England, tennis is played mainly at local tennis clubs, as much for its social aspects as for sport.

The sport with the greatest number of regular participants in England is angling (fishing). Hunting as such is not a big sport in England, but fox hunting has its followers. Fox hunters gather in groups of twenty or thirty riders on horses, dressed in their pinks (pink coats). The hunt rides out with a pack of hounds (usually beagles or bloodhounds) to pursue the fox. The dogs actually catch and kill the fox. Campaigners against fox hunting protest that it is a cruelty "sport" that should be banned. Hunters argue that foxes are pests, that hunting them is the most humane way of killing them, and that fox hunting is a traditional countryside activity. Although fox hunting has long been considered an activity for the upper classes, it now includes people from all walks of life.

Horse racing has a dedicated following among people from all walks of life. Some of the biggest events of the British sporting calendar are

Tennis player Tim Henman celebrates a triumph at the 2002 Wimbledon Championship. Many hope that Henman will win at Wimbledon for England someday. England has not won a male tournament at Wimbledon since 1936.

the Grand National (a long-distance steeplechase race), Ascot (a week of races and a great social occasion), and the Epsom Derby (equally, a great social occasion). Millions of people who otherwise never gamble put a small bet on the Grand National.

The Television and Radio Media

The British Broadcasting Corporation (BBC) was founded in 1927. The BBC is financed mainly by the annual license fee. Everyone in Britain with a television or radio (meaning virtually everyone) has to pay the TV license. The BBC had a monopoly on all radio and television broadcasting in Britain until 1954, when the Independent Television Authority (later renamed the Independent Broadcasting Authority, or IBA) was established. The IBA was set up to provide commercial television and radio broadcasting, financed mainly by advertising, which the BBC, as a public broadcaster, does not have. Until recently, there were two BBC television channels (BBC 1 and BBC 2) and four radio channels (BBC 1, 2, 3, and 4). The BBC now has two other television channels (BBC 3 and BBC 4), through satellite and digital transmission. It also has regional television and radio channels within England and for Wales and Northern Ireland. The BBC World Service (radio) started broadcasting in 1932 (when it was called the Empire Service). It now broadcasts programs in more than thirty languages to an estimated 150 to 200 million listeners worldwide. In 1997, the BBC started a twenty-four-hour news channel.

The Bush House, headquarters of the BBC. The English have affectionately nicknamed their famous broadcasting corporation "Beeb" and "Auntie."

Independent television (ITV) in Britain is composed of a group of private companies that broadcast in competition with the BBC. The first ITV broadcast was in 1954. Early on, the ITV programs were much more "popular" than those on the BBC. (The BBC had to broadcast programs in the public interest, similar to Public Service Radio in the United States.) The main difference now between the various ITV broadcasters and the BBC is that the BBC still carries no advertising, whereas the ITV companies do. Now, independent satellite and cable broadcasters also offer dozens of channels for an annual subscription charge.

The Newspaper Press

The big daily newspapers in Britain are read around the country. There are two informally classified kinds of daily national newspapers: quality broadsheets and tabloids. The broadsheets (named because the pages are large) have higher-quality information and news coverage. *The Times* (founded 1785), *The Guardian* (1821), *The Daily Telegraph* (1855), and *The Daily Mail* (1896) are the biggest-selling broadsheets. The tabloids (smaller in size than the broadsheets) sell many more copies than the broadsheets. *The Sun* and *The Daily Mirror* are the biggest-selling tabloids. In addition to the national press, there are thousands of local newspapers published around the country.

The National Health Service

In July 1948, the National Health Service (NHS) was established. The NHS provides a service of free health care to everyone in Britain (except for charges for prescriptions and some non-NHS services). In England, the service

A collection of English newspapers headline Princess Diana's fatal car crash on August 31, 1997. Diana's death shocked the world.

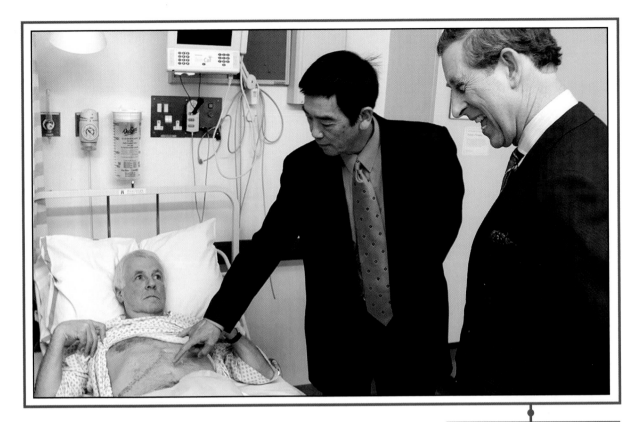

is structured on three levels: local general practitioners (GPs; family doctors) and nurses in local surgeries (clinics) for primary care, specialist hospital services for secondary care, and the specialist health authorities that provide health services to the whole population of England (for example, the National Blood Authority). Demand for health services has always increased faster than resources to meet the demand. People sometimes wait more than a year for a nonemergency operation. Reducing waiting times for operations is now a priority for the NHS.

Many people now prefer to pay a monthly charge for private health insurance, for the convenience of immediate hospital treatment when they need it. Private hospitals and clinics generally have more pleasant surroundings, with higher-quality accommodations and food, than the public NHS hospitals. The quality of clinical care, however, is not particularly better than that provided by the NHS. Many doctors work for both the NHS and private clinics and hospitals.

EDUCATION AND WORK IN ENGLAND

U ntil quite recently, most English students left school at age sixteen to go to work. Only a minority went to college or university. That is now changing. More students are going on to higher education. One reason for this is that England has become a middle-class country. Higher education is part of the middle-class culture. Another reason is that young people are looking for better paid jobs that require a college degree. When they do go to work, the English work longer hours than most other countries in Europe. The official maximum working hours in a week in the United Kingdom—forty-eight—are the highest in the European Union.

The English Education System

Schooling is compulsory in England for all children from the ages of five to sixteen. There are two kinds of schools in England: state schools (which are public) and public schools (which are private!). The state schools are financed and run by the government. State schools do not charge parents for their children's education. Primary education is up to the age of eleven. In secondary education, between the ages of eleven and sixteen, schools generally accept children of all abilities. These are comprehensive schools. There are others, however, called grammar schools, that only accept students on the basis of an

Pictured at left, Eton College students walk to class in their uniforms. Many famous people, including writers Henry Fielding, George Orwell, and Ian Fleming, attended Eton College. Pictured above, a small class at Tacolneston First School learns about world religions. Village schools are often very small and give more individual attention to students.

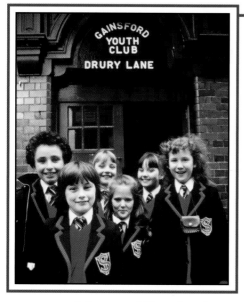

entrance exam. Secondary schools are mainly coeducational (girls and boys together). Grammar schools tend to be either girls or boys only.

Parents pay fees for children who go to public schools. Most are boarding schools, where students live during term times. The first public schools were just for boys. Girls-only schools started toward the late nineteenth century. Public schools tend to offer a wider range of nonacademic activities and sports than state schools. It may still be true, too, that the best universities (Oxford and Cambridge) look to public schools first for the best students. England's two most prestigious public schools are Harrow School (founded in 1571) and Eton College (founded in 1440). The oldest English public school is Winchester College, founded in 1394. Charterhouse (1611), St. Paul's School (1509), and Rugby School (1567) all have traditions and records of academic excellence stretching back hundreds of years.

The National Curriculum

All state schools follow a fixed national curriculum of courses in eleven subjects (such as English, mathematics, geography, art, science, and so on). Public schools tend to follow the curriculum but with a greater range of subjects. Students take national exams at age sixteen and eighteen. The first are for the General Certificate of Secondary Education (GCSEs). Students are tested on subjects in the national curriculum from the previous two years (years ten and eleven, ages fourteen to sixteen). Up to ten subjects may be taken. The average is six.

To go up to the next level, students have to pass their GCSEs with a C grade or better. In years twelve and thirteen (ages sixteen to eighteen), students study up to four or five subjects (usually three) before taking General Certificate of Education Advanced (GCE "A") exams. Some subjects are only studied for one year for the GCE "Advanced Subsidiary" ("AS") exam. Students' grades in the GCE "A" or "AS" exams are used as qualifications to go on to a university.

Universities and Colleges

There are eighty-nine universities in Britain, as well as colleges and other institutions of higher education (including teacher training colleges). To apply for a place at a university, students go through the Universities and Colleges Admissions Service (UCAS). Applicants choose up to six universities (and specific courses), which they enter on the UCAS application form (without stating a preference). The UCAS sends the details of each applicant to the universities. The universities evaluate each applicant (sometimes requiring an interview). They then either offer a place at the university to the applicant or they reject him or her. The offer depends on how well the student does on his or her GCE "A" or "AS" exams. A candidate can accept two offers: a first choice, plus an additional one in case the first one is rejected. Universities make their final decision on a candidate after the GCE exam results are published in late August. Universities must accept all applicants who have achieved the results required by them. Universities may accept candidates who have not achieved the results required, at the discretion of the university. Any applicants who do not get a place at a university or who apply too late (after July 1) may find a place on the list of university vacancies for specific courses. In that case, applicants negotiate a place directly with the university.

The 2001 Census for England and Wales revealed that 20 percent of the adult population of England had graduated from a university or other institution of higher education. The number of college or university graduates in England is nowhere near the number in the United States. That is partly because most people in Britain leave school at age sixteen or eighteen to find a job. Also, secondary school qualifications (GCSEs and GCEs) are accepted as the usual standard of ability by many employers. Going to college or university was also considered more of a class-oriented situation; working-class people worked, and upper-class people went to university. Nowadays, it is much more common for young people to go on to university or higher education after GCEs. The working-class distinction has also virtually disappeared. Most English people have become middle class.

Cambridge and Oxford Universities stand apart from all other universities in England. Besides their long history and international reputation as centers of academic excellence, they are structured in a different way than other British universities. Both Oxford and Cambridge are composed of individual colleges. Students are accepted by a particular college to spend their university life in that college. The oldest Cambridge college is Peterhouse, founded in 1284 (just over 200 years after the Norman Conquest).

The Eurostar arrives at a station. The Eurostar is a high-speed train that connects London with Lille, Paris, and Brussels. The train is so fast, traveling 208 mph (334.7 km/h), that a ride from London to Brussels takes a little less than two and a half hours.

The first Oxford colleges were even earlier: University College (1249), Merton College (1263), and Balliol College (1263).

Work

In the early years of England's history, people farmed. Later on, after the Industrial Revolution, they manufactured. Now they "manage." In the 2001 census of the population, 15 percent of people in the United Kingdom said they worked as "senior officials" (executives) in management. Of all kinds of employment, management jobs employed the most people (according to the census). Around 13 percent of people said they worked in "administrative and secretarial" jobs. Another 13 percent claimed to work as "associate professionals" and technical workers (lab technicians, nurses, artists, and so on). "Skilled tradesmen" (plumbers, electricians, welders, and so on) accounted for another 12 percent of working people, "professionals" (consultants, bankers, teachers, and so on) made up 11 percent, and people in elementary occupations (hotel workers, cleaners, waiters, and so on) accounted for 12 percent. Agriculture and farming only account for about 1 percent of people working in the

United Kingdom today. The remaining 23 percent of the working population were self-employed or employed in other kinds of work (for example, part-time work).

Women have become a much more integrated part of the labor force. In 1955, 46 percent of all adult women in the UK worked paid jobs. By 1995, that had risen to 67 percent. In 1956, women were 31 percent of the total UK labor force and, in 1995, 42 percent. Many more women than men, however, work either part-time or low-level jobs. About 23 percent of all jobs in the UK are part-time, 80 percent of which are filled by women. Men account for only about 20 percent of all part-time employment. Only about 25 percent of women with children hold full-time jobs, but more and more are working part-time. Women account for about 90 percent of nurses and midwives in the UK, 75 percent of all clerical and secretarial jobs, almost 66 percent of all teachers, but less than 33 percent of all professional (executive) and managerial jobs. Men still dominate the workplace. Women provide the greatest source of flexible labor for part-time or occasional work.

Postwar Industrial Decline

England used to manufacture everything from trains to bridges, ships, typewriters, bicycles, and clothing. It mined all the coal it needed to fuel all those industries. "Made in England" was a label of quality and prestige. After World War II, but particularly from the 1960s onward, manufacturing industries in Britain declined. Most coal mines were shut down in the 1970s. Shipyards closed. Whole towns were ruined by the closure of steel mills. Most things that Britain used to make could now be made more cheaply in other parts of the world, such as Japan, South Korea, China, Turkey, and Brazil. Britain's biggest manufacturing industries today are food and drink and motor vehicles (cars and trucks). The value of food and drink production in 1997 was £63 billion

This is the Motorola Electronics Factory in Swindon. Despite the decline of manufacturing companies, unemployment and inflation remain low.

An aerial view shows London's financial center. London is an important center for commerce and politics in England as well as the world. The city is bustling with many industries, shops, and people. There are over 7 million people living in Greater London.

($100 billion), and the value of of automobile production was £31 billion ($50 billion). Before World War II, most cars made in Britain were made by British companies. Today, all the cars and trucks made in Britain are made by foreign companies, either Japanese, Korean, American, or European.

Rise of the Service Industries

Britain has replaced a lot of its manufacturing with service industries such as banking and finance, retailing, tourism, health care, property development, information technology services (but not equipment), and consultancy. Service industries now account for 75 percent of the total labor force of around 28 million people in England. Manufacturing industries account for another 24 percent, and agriculture employs just 1 percent. More people work in offices and shops (retailing) than at any time in Britain's history. Call centers have become a big new source of employment in Britain. These are huge centers at which hundreds of people are on the phone all day, every day, either taking calls to give people advice about something or making calls to sell everything from windows to insurance. Telecommuting (working mainly from home and communicating by phone or e-mail) has also become a new trend. In 2003, an estimated 2.2 million people in the UK were telecommuting.

The City of London: Financial Heartbeat of England

The old square mile of London built by the Romans is now the City of London. Thousands of banks, insurance companies, and stockbrokers have their offices within this small area of London. It is one of the great financial centers of the world, the center of the most valuable service industries in the country, and the financial heart of Britain. Hundreds of thousands of people commute into the City, as it is called, every day. By night and on weekends, only a few thousand people live there. During the working week, it becomes a beehive of activity. London itself is the greatest center of employment in Britain. Trains, the Tube (the subway), and cars and buses transport millions of London workers to and from the suburbs. Many people spend their whole working lives as London commuters.

Integrating with Europe

Since 1973, Britain has been a member of the European Union (originally called the European Common Market, then the European Community, now the European Union). This has brought workers in Britain much closer to their continental European neighbors. The business centers of Europe, such as Paris, Milan, Madrid, and Frankfurt, are all within two hours' flying time from London. Since 2002, most EU countries (but not Britain) have adopted the common EU currency called the euro to replace their national currencies. This has made it much easier to do business among EU countries. Many businesspeople now travel back and forth to Europe as easily as they take the train to work. As members of the EU, British citizens have the right to live and work in any EU country, without restriction. It is much easier and more common now than it ever was for a British person to spend a few months or years working and living in another European country. There is still a very particular English or British working culture, but that is becoming gradually more European.

ENGLAND
AT A GLANCE

HISTORY

In the Stone Age (70,000 to 3000 BC), the inhabitants of Britain lived by hunting and picking wild food. Tribes of people known as Iberians started farming and making tools around 3000 BC. The huge stone circle called Stonehenge was built around 2000 BC. Invaders from mainland Europe, the Celts, moved into Britain around 700 BC. The Romans pushed the Celts to the west when they arrived in AD 43.

The Romans ruled Britain until AD 410. They built long, straight roads, introduced Christianity into Britain, and settled what we know today as England. After they left in AD 410, tribes of Angles, Saxons, and Jutes from northern Europe invaded and settled. These Anglo-Saxons were the first English people. In 597, Augustine led a mission from Rome to convert the English to Christianity. Over the next 100 years, every English king was converted. Starting at the end of the eighth century, Vikings from Norway and Denmark attacked the northeast coast of England. They eventually settled in that area, called the Danelaw, under an agreement with the Anglo-Saxon king Alfred the Great (849–899).

In 1066, William, Duke of Normandy, invaded from France, defeating the English king Harold at the Battle of Hastings on the south coast. William the Conqueror was crowned King William I. The Norman invasion marked the beginning of English history as a single nation under a single crown. In 1215, the document known as the Magna Carta established the principles of fair justice for all English people. It was the origin of Parliament and democratic government. Between 1348 and 1350, the plague killed around one-third of the population.

Henry VIII (1457–1509) established the national church (the Church of England), breaking the church's ties with the pope in Rome. In 1543, Henry VIII united England and Wales under a single crown. During the reign of Elizabeth I (1533–1603), English explorers established the great strength of England as a maritime power around the world. In 1588, the English navy defeated the Armada (navy) sent by the Catholic king of Spain, Phillip II (1527–1598), to invade England. The Pilgrims sailed for America in 1620, to escape religious persecution.

112

In 1665, plague returned to England. The next year (1666), the Great Fire of London burned for three days, destroying tens of thousands of buildings.

In 1707, Scotland's own Parliament was abolished. From then until 1999, Scotland would be represented at Parliament in London. The political union of Scotland and England created the United Kingdom of Great Britain. In 1776, America declared its independence from Britain. The Industrial Revolution in England developed from the late 1700s through the 1800s. Millions of people moved away from farming to work in the industrial towns and cities.

By 1900, 80 percent of the population was living in towns and cities. In the twentieth century, Germany threatened to invade England in World War II. Winston Churchill (1874–1965) led the country to victory as one of Britain's greatest prime ministers and statesmen. On the death of her father, King George VI (1895–1952), Elizabeth II (1926–) became queen. Britain became a member of the European Economic Community (now the European Union) in 1973. In August 1997, Diana, princess of Wales and wife of Prince Charles, was killed in a car crash in Paris. In 2002, Elizabeth II's fiftieth year as queen was celebrated throughout Britain.

ECONOMY

The Industrial Revolution in Britain during the eighteenth and nineteenth centuries made Britain a world power. Its strength was in textiles, machinery, shipbuilding, coal mining, and engineering. World War II reduced Britain's manufacturing abilities. Many of its important industrial areas were destroyed by German bombing. The economy took thirty years to recover to a degree at which it could compete with other world powers. In 1973, Britain became a member of the European Economic Community (EEC; now called the European Union, or EU). Membership in the EEC/EU helped British industry compete with other EEC/EU member countries. The economy was boosted by the discovery and development of natural gas and oil fields in the North Sea, in the 1960s. Production from those offshore fields has made Britain one of the world's largest producers of oil and gas.

During the 1980s, the conservative government began to privatize many industries that were publicly owned by the state. They included coal mining, steel, automobiles, and energy production. In the late 1990s, the publicly owned railway network (British Rail) was privatized. The railways are now run by private train operators. The aim of privatization was to make those industries more efficient. One of the results was the closure of production facilities, especially in coal mining and the steel industry. The most important remaining manufacturing industries in the north of England are food processing, brewing, chemicals, textiles, glass, automobiles, and paper products. In the south, the main industries are pharmaceuticals, computers and microelectronics, and automobiles.

Throughout the twentieth century, farming declined from being a major contributor to the British economy to being a minor but still strategically important sector. Subsidies from the EU have helped farmers stay in business, but their profitability has declined to very low levels. In 2002, the average annual income of British farmers was less than £5,594 ($10,000). Fishing used to be an important industry. Quotas imposed by the EU that restrict the amounts of fish that can be caught and declining fish populations in nearby waters have greatly reduced the British fishing industry.

Britain is now mainly a services economy. Service industries (banking and financial services, retailing, tourism, and leisure) account for around three-quarters of the British economy. London has been a major world financial center for many years. Tourism has grown rapidly to become an important contributor to the British economy. Services related to high-technology sectors (the Internet, mobile communications, and so on) are becoming increasingly important.

GOVERNMENT AND POLITICS

England is one of four countries within the United Kingdom. The others are Wales, Scotland, and Northern Ireland. England is governed as part of the United Kingdom's system of parliamentary democracy and constitutional monarchy. The sovereign (reigning monarch) is the head of state. Since 1953, the reigning monarch has been Queen Elizabeth II. The sovereign is head of the judiciary (legal system), commander in chief of all the armed forces, and supreme governor of the Church of England. The prime minister is head of the democratically elected government. There is no written constitution as there is in the United States. The British constitution is the combination of British laws and practices that have arisen over hundreds of years of parliamentary government. Since it is unwritten, the "constitution" is flexible and changes constantly according to new laws and practices. Parliament is the two-house legislative assembly, where legislation and government policies are debated and made into law. Parliament is made up of the House of Commons, the House of Lords (the upper house), and the sovereign. The sovereign gives royal assent to (approves) all laws after they have been passed by the Commons and the Lords. (The last time a sovereign vetoed a piece of legislation was in 1707.) The two houses are held at Westminster in Central London.

The Commons has 658 members of Parliament (MPs) elected by local constituencies (the places they represent). MPs serve for the duration of the Parliament's term. A term of Parliament lasts five years unless the government calls an election earlier. The Commons is the center of parliamentary power in Britain. It makes laws that are reviewed and debated by the House of Lords before they are given royal assent by the sovereign. Most MPs who sit in the Commons are from the three dominant political parties: Labour, Conservative, and Liberal Democrat. Minor parties include Plaid Cymru (Welsh Nationalist), Scottish National, Ulster Unionist (Northern Ireland), Democratic Unionist (Northern Ireland), Social Democratic and Labour (Northern Ireland).

The House of Lords is made up of peers and their female equivalent, peeresses (members of the nobility), some of whom have inherited their title (hereditary peers) and some of whom have been awarded their title by the reigning monarch (life peers); the two archbishops (of Canterbury and York) and the twenty-four most senior bishops of the Church of England; and the judges of the two supreme courts in Britain (the Court of Appeal and the High Court of Justice). The main function of the House of Lords is to review and debate issues related to new legislation passed to it from the House of Commons.

The party with the greatest number of elected MPs (Labour or Conservative since 1937) is officially invited by the sovereign to form the government. The leader of the party is traditionally appointed by the sovereign to be prime minister. The governing party originates almost all new legislation debated by the Commons. It also forms a cabinet that is made up of senior ministers chosen by the prime minister from among the party's elected MPs. The cabinet formulates policy that is the basis for debate and legislation in the Commons. The main minority party (so far either Labour or Conservative) is the government's official opposition. The opposition has a shadow cabinet that formulates that party's official policies. Its main objective is to challenge the policies of the governing party in order to gain power in the next election.

TIMELINE

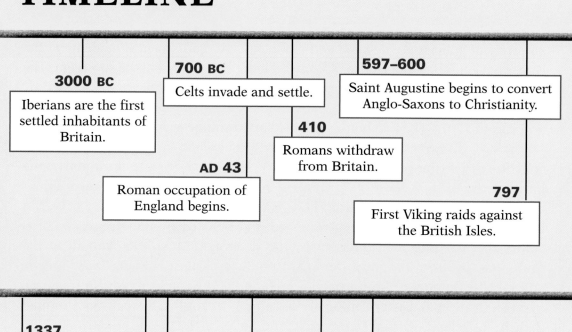

3000 BC
Iberians are the first settled inhabitants of Britain.

700 BC
Celts invade and settle.

AD 43
Roman occupation of England begins.

410
Romans withdraw from Britain.

597–600
Saint Augustine begins to convert Anglo-Saxons to Christianity.

797
First Viking raids against the British Isles.

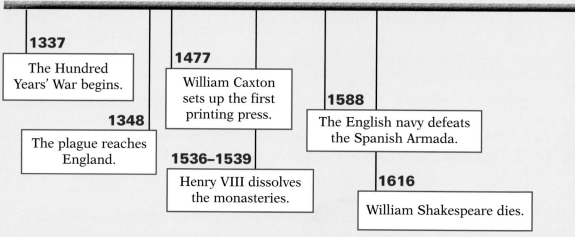

1337
The Hundred Years' War begins.

1348
The plague reaches England.

1477
William Caxton sets up the first printing press.

1536–1539
Henry VIII dissolves the monasteries.

1588
The English navy defeats the Spanish Armada.

1616
William Shakespeare dies.

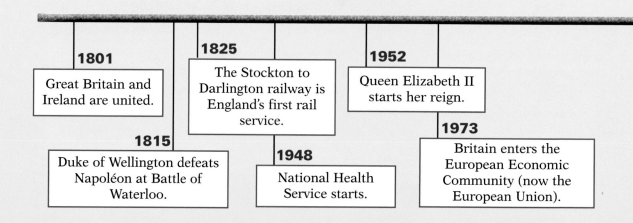

1801
Great Britain and Ireland are united.

1815
Duke of Wellington defeats Napoléon at Battle of Waterloo.

1825
The Stockton to Darlington railway is England's first rail service.

1948
National Health Service starts.

1952
Queen Elizabeth II starts her reign.

1973
Britain enters the European Economic Community (now the European Union).

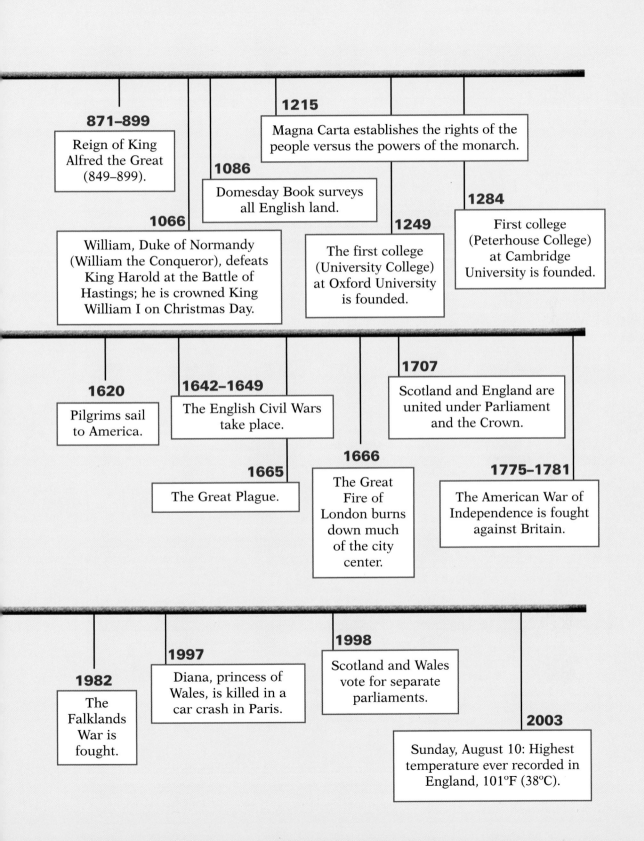

871–899

Reign of King Alfred the Great (849–899).

1066

William, Duke of Normandy (William the Conqueror), defeats King Harold at the Battle of Hastings; he is crowned King William I on Christmas Day.

1086

Domesday Book surveys all English land.

1215

Magna Carta establishes the rights of the people versus the powers of the monarch.

1249

The first college (University College) at Oxford University is founded.

1284

First college (Peterhouse College) at Cambridge University is founded.

1620

Pilgrims sail to America.

1642–1649

The English Civil Wars take place.

1665

The Great Plague.

1666

The Great Fire of London burns down much of the city center.

1707

Scotland and England are united under Parliament and the Crown.

1775–1781

The American War of Independence is fought against Britain.

1982

The Falklands War is fought.

1997

Diana, princess of Wales, is killed in a car crash in Paris.

1998

Scotland and Wales vote for separate parliaments.

2003

Sunday, August 10: Highest temperature ever recorded in England, 101°F (38°C).

ENGLAND

Shetland Islands

Legend
Coal
Agriculture
Manufacturing/Steel
Automotive
Railway Manufacturing

Outer Hebrides
The Little Minch
The Minch
SCOTLAND
Aberdeen
ATLANTIC OCEAN
NORTH SEA
Fife Ness
Glasgow
Fifth of Forth
St Abb's Head
Berwick-upon-Tweed
NORTHERN IRELAND
Belfast
Wooler
Bamburgh
Morpeth
Carlisle
Newcastle upon Tyne
South Shields
Sunderland
Silloth
Durham
Hartlepool
Workington
Frizington
Penrith
Brew
Darlington
South Bank
Gosforth
Tebay
Middlesbrough
Millom
Richmond
Isle of Man
Northallerton
Scarborough
Barrow-in-Furness
Morecambe
Filey
Flamborough Head
IRELAND
IRISH SEA
Fleetwood
Lancaster
Harrogate
York
Wetwang
Bridlington
Blackpool
Preston
Halifax
Leeds
Kingston upon Hull
Lytham St Anne's
Bolton
Southport
Patrington
Liverpool
Salford
Manchester
Scunthorpe
Great Grimsby
Stockport
Sheffield
NORTH SEA
Chester
Crewe
Chesterfield
Mablethorpe
Stoke-on-Trent
Lincoln
Skegness
Derby
Nottingham
Boston
The Wash
Shrewsbury
Telford
Stafford
Grantham
Cromer
North Channel
St Georges Channel
Oakham
Crowland
King's Lynn
Norwich
Birmingham
Coventry
Peterborough
Great Yarmouth
Worcester
Royal L. Spa
Thetford
Lowestoft
WALES
Hereford
Upton
Evesham
Bedford
Cambridge
Gloucester
Cheltenham
Milton Keynes
Ipswich
Caldey I.
Thornbury
Oxford
St Albans
Harlow
Cardiff
Bristol
Swindon
Reading
LONDON
CELTIC SEA
Bristol Channel
Bath
Hartland Point
Weston-Super-Mare
Basingstoke
Bracknell
Grays
Southend-on-Sea
Clovelly
Barnstaple
Taunton
Winchester
Guildford
Maidstone
Ramsgate
Bude
Great Torrington
Salisbury
Royal Tunbridge Wells
Dover
BELGIUM
Trevose Head
Launceston
Exeter
Honiton
Southampton
Eastleigh
Crawley
Hastings
Newquay
Dawlish
Dorchester
Poole
Gosport
Chichester
St Ives
Liskeard
Kingswear
Bournemouth
Isle of Wight
Worthing
Eastbourne
Truro
Plymouth
Portsmouth
Brighton
FRANCE
Isles of Scilly
Penzance
Falmouth
Salcombe
Kingsbridge
Guernsey
St Catherine's Point
Start Point
ENGLISH CHANNEL
Strait of Dover

ECONOMIC FACT SHEET

GDP in US$: $1,500 billion (est. 2002); per capita: $25,300 (est. 2002)

Currency: UK£ ($1.60 = £1)

Workforce: 29.7 million. Agriculture 1%, industry 25%, services 74%

Major Agricultural Products: Cereals, oilseed, potatoes, other vegetables, cattle, sheep, poultry, fish

Major Exports: In 2001, £191.5 billion ($306 billion); in 2002, £187 billion ($299 billion). In 2002, electrical and optical equipment, £45 billion ($72 billion); transport equipment/vehicles, £31 billion ($50 billion); chemicals and chemical products, £29 billion ($46 billion); audio/video/communications equipment, £20 billion ($32 billion); miscellaneous machinery and equipment, £16 billion ($26 billion)

Major Imports: In 2001, £230 billion ($368 billion). In 2002:, £227 billion ($363 billion). In 2002, electrical and optical equipment, £45 billion ($72 billion); transport equipment/vehicles, £44 billion ($70 billion); chemicals and chemical products, £25 billion ($40 billion); food and drink, £15 billion ($24 billion)

Significant Trading Partners:

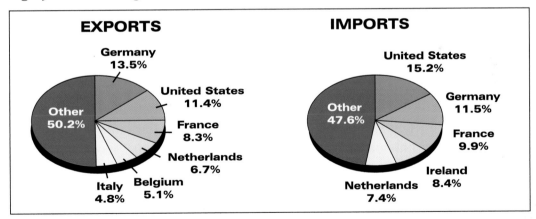

Inflation: 2.5%

Rate of Unemployment: 5%

Highways: 230,394 miles (371,603 km)

Railroads: 10,464 miles (16,878 km)

Waterways: 1,984 miles (3,200 km)

Airports: 470 (with paved runways: 334)

POLITICAL FACT SHEET

Official Country Name: The United Kingdom of Great Britain and Northern Ireland (England, Wales, Scotland, and Northern Ireland)

Official Flag: United Kingdom: the Union Flag, commonly called the Union Jack; blue with the red cross of Saint George (patron saint of England)

edged in white superimposed on the diagonal red cross of Saint Patrick (patron saint of Ireland), which is superimposed on the diagonal white cross of Saint Andrew (patron saint of Scotland)

England: Saint George's cross on white background

National Anthem (England): "Land of Hope and Glory"

> Land of hope and glory,
> Mother of the free,
> How shall we extole thee,
> Who are born of thee,
> Wider and still wider,

> Shall thy bounds be set,
> God who made the mighty,
> Make thee mightier yet!,
> God who made thee mighty,
> Make thee mightier yet!

Government: Head of State: Her Majesty Queen Elizabeth II since 1953; Prime Minister: The Right Honorable Tony Blair since 1997. Parliament: Last (2001) election result: Labour Party, 412 seats (62.5% of seats; 40.7% of votes); Tony Blair, party leader. Conservative Party, 166 seats (25.2% of seats; 31.7% of votes); William Hague/Ian Duncan Smith, party leader (Ian Duncan Smith took over). Liberal Democrat Party: 52 seats (7.9% of seats; 18.3% of votes); Charles Kennedy, party leader. Others: 28 seats (4.2% of seats; 9.3% of votes). Altogether, 78 parties put forward 3,319 candidates for election, of which 658 were elected.

2001 Electorate/Registered Voters: United Kingdom: 44,401,238 electorate, 26,366,992 total vote, 59.4% turnout; England: 36,990,780 electorate, 21,870,488 total vote, 59.1% turnout; Northern Ireland: 1,191,009 electorate, 810,381 total vote, 68% turnout; Scotland: 3,983,306 electorate, 2,313,581 total vote, 58.1% turnout; Wales: 2,236,143 electorate, 1,372,542 total vote, 61.4% turnout.

CULTURAL FACT SHEET

Official Languages: English; also Welsh (about 26 percent of the population of Wales) and Scots Gaelic (about 60,000 speakers in Scotland)

Major Religions: UK: Anglican and Roman Catholic (about 40 million), Islam (1.5 million), Presbyterian (about 800,000), Methodist (about 700,000), Hindu (about 500,000), Sikh (about 350,000), Jewish (about 350,000)

Capital: London, population 6.6 million; Greater London, 7.6 million

Population: UK: 59.8 million (est. 2002); England: 48 million (est. 2002)

Ethnic Groups: UK: English, 81.5%; Scottish, 9.6%; Irish, 2.4%; Welsh, 1.9%; Ulster/Northern Ireland, 1.8%; Afro-Caribbean, 0.8%; Indian, Pakistani, and other, 0.2%

Life Expectancy: 78 years men; 81 years women

Time: Greenwich Mean Time (GMT); British Summer Time (BST) from late March until late October is GMT plus one hour

Literacy Rate: (Defined as the percent of the population ages 15 and over who have completed five or more years of schooling): 99% (est. 2002)

Cultural Leaders:

Visual Arts: Thomas Gainsborough (1727–1788), J. M. W. Turner (1775–1851), John Constable (1776–1837), Francis Bacon (1909–1992), Lucian Freud (1922–)

Literature: William Shakespeare (1564–1616), Ben Jonson (1573–1637), John Milton (1608–1674), William Wordsworth (1770–1850), Jane Austen (1775–1817), Charles Dickens (1812–1870), J. K. Rowling (Harry Potter) (1965–)

Music/Dance: Sir William Gilbert (1836–1911), Sir Arthur Sullivan (1842–1900), Sir Edward Elgar (1857–1934), Ralph Vaughan Williams (1872–1958), Sir Benjamin Britten (1913–1976), Dame Margot Fonteyn (1919–1991), The Beatles, The Rolling Stones

National Holidays and Festivals

January 1: **New Year's Day**
April: **Good Friday**
April: **Easter Monday**
May: **May Bank Holiday**
End of May (Mon.): **Spring Bank Holiday**

End of August (Monday): **Summer Bank Holiday**
December 25: **Christmas**
December 26: **Boxing Day**

GLOSSARY

adulterate (uh-DUL-tur-ate): To add something to food, usually to increase its weight (and price).

adulterous (uh-DUL-ter-uss): Unfaithfulness in marriage.

allegory (AL-egg-ory): A description or narrative of something that has a second, deeper meaning.

celibacy (SELL-ih-buh-see): Being both unmarried and sexually inactive.

chivalry (SHI-vuhl-ree): The practice of ideal human behavior (courtesy, bravery, faithfulness, etc.) from the Middle Ages.

collier (KOLL-ee-yer): A small ship used to carry freight (usually coal).

colloquially (kull-OH-kwee-ull-ee): Familiar or informal.

culinary (KULL-in-eh-ree): Relating to cooking.

cull (KULL): To reduce the size of a herd or group of animals by killing selected individuals.

doctrine (DOK-trin): Principles and beliefs.

feudal (FEW-duhl): Medieval system in which nobility (lords) owned inherited land that was farmed by serfs.

fishmonger (FISH-mong-er): A person (or shop) that sells fish.

forerunner (FOR-run-ner): The first of its kind; a pioneer.

greengrocer (GREEN-groh-sher): A person (or shop) that sells fresh fruit and vegetables.

hedgerow (HEDJ-roh): A row of shrubs planted as a hedge.

iconoclastic (eye-kon-oh-CLASS-tik): Nonconformist, unconventional, breaking from tradition.

indomitable (in-DOM-ih-ta-buhl): Someone or something that cannot be conquered.

linguistic (ling-GWIST-ik): To do with language.

liturgy (LI-tur-jee): The complete form and format of ritual in public worship, set out in a single document.

madrigal (MAD-rig-uhl): A poetic song in verse, originally from Italy, particularly from the fourteenth to sixteenth centuries.

martyr (MAR-ter): Someone who dies or is killed for his or her religious beliefs.

ordain (or-DANE): To appoint someone ceremonially to a position of authority in the church (especially a priest).

ordination (or-di-NAY-shun): The ceremony of appointing someone to a position of authority in the church.

pagan (PAY-gun): Pre-Christian, with pre-Christian beliefs, gods, etc.

prestigious (pres-TEE-jus): Highly valued.

rural (RUHR-uhl): Of the countryside.

sanctuary (SANK-chu-ehr-ee): A refuge; a place where wild animals are protected.

secular (SEK-u-lur): Nonreligious.

serf (SERF): A laborer who works for a feudal master (usually a lord).

sonnet (SOHN-et): A fourteen-line poem with a specific rhyme scheme.

staple (STAY-pul): Any main food(s) eaten ordinarily.

subjugation (sub-ju-GAY-shun): Oppression.

supremacy (suh-PREM-uh-see): Leadership over all.

temperate (TEMP-ur-ut): Mild (as in climate or weather).

FOR MORE INFORMATION

British Tourist Authority (BTA)
551 Fifth Avenue, 7th Floor
New York, NY 10176-0799
(212) 986-2200
(800) GO-2-BRITAIN ((468) 274-8246)
Web site: http://www.visitbritain.com

The National Trust
36 Queen Anne's Circle
London SW1H 9AS
0870 609 5380
Web site: http://www.nationaltrust.org.uk

Web Sites

Due to the changing nature of Internet links, the Rosen Publishing Group, Inc., has developed an online list of Web sites related to the subject of this book. This site is updated regularly. Please use this link to access the list:

http://www.rosenlinks.com/pswc/engl

FOR FURTHER READING

Black, Jeremy. *A New History of England.* Stroud, UK: Sutton Publishing Ltd., 2000.

Brabbs, Derry. *England's Heritage.* London: Weidenfeld & Nicolson, 2003.

Bryson, Bill. *Notes from a Small Island.* London: Black Swan, 1996.

Hobsbawm, Eric. *Industry and Empire: From 1750 to the Present Day.* London: Penguin Books, 1999.

Hoskins, W. G. *The Making of the English Landscape.* London: Penguin Books, 1999.

Paxman, Jeremy. *The English: A Portrait of a People.* London: Michael Joseph, 1998.

Raban, Jonathan. *Coasting: A Private Journey.* London: Picador, 1995.

Schama, Simon. *A History of Britain.* London: BBC Consumer Publishing, 2000.

Wiener, Martin Joel. *English Culture and the Decline of the Industrial Spirit, 1850–1980.* Cambridge, UK: Cambridge University Press, 1982.

BIBLIOGRAPHY

Barber, Richard. *Myths and Legends of the British Isles.* Woodbridge, UK: Boydell and Brewer, 2000.

Bett, Henry. *English Legends.* London: B. T. Batsford Ltd., 1950.

Crystal, David. *The Cambridge Encyclopedia of the English Language.* Cambridge, UK: The Cambridge University Press, 1995.

Crystal, David. *The English Language.* London: Penguin Books, 2002.

Daniell, Christopher. *A Traveller's History of England.* Moreton-in-Marsh, UK: The Windrush Press, 2001.

Delderfield, Eric R., ed. *Kings and Queens of England and Great Britain.* Newton Abbot, UK: David & Charles Ltd., 1981.

Drabble, Margaret, ed. *The Oxford Companion to English Literature.* Oxford, UK: Oxford University Press, 1996.

Evans, Sir Benjamin Ifor. *A Short History of English Literature.* Harmandsworth, UK: Penguin Books Ltd./Pelican, 1960.

Gaunt, William. *English Painting: A Concise History.* London: Thames and Hudson, 1991.

Godfrey-Faussett, Charlie. *England.* Bath, UK: Footprint Handbooks, 2003.

Hartley, Dorothy. *Food in England.* London: Little, Brown and Co., 1999.

Hole, Christina. *English Custom and Usage.* London: B. T. Batsford Ltd., 1944.

Hunt, Robert. *Cornish Folklore.* Redruth, UK: Tor Mark Press, 2000.

Johnson, Edward Hotspur. *Yorkshire-English Dictionary.* London: Abson Books London, 1990.

Kirkpatrick, Betty. *The Little Book of Cockney Rhyming Slang.* London: Michael O'Mara Books, 2002.

Phillipps, Kenneth. *A Glossary of the Cornish Dialect.* Padstow, UK: Tabb House, 1993.

Pullar, Philippa. *Consuming Passions: A History of English Food and Appetite.* London: Book Club Associates/ Hamish Hamilton Ltd., 1970.

Rogers, Pat, ed. *The Oxford Illustrated History of English Literature.* London: Oxford University Press, 2001.

Simpson, Jacqueline, and Steve Roud. *Oxford Dictionary of English Folklore.* Oxford, UK: Oxford University Press, 2001.

Trevelyan, George Macaulay. *A Shortened History of England.* Harmandsworth, UK: Penguin Books Ltd., 1959.

Watkin, David. *English Architecture.* London: Thames and Hudson, 1985.

PRIMARY SOURCE IMAGE LIST

● ● ●

Page 9 (top): *The Port of London*, circa nineteenth century, by Thomas Allom. Housed in the Victoria & Albert Museum in London.

Page 24: *Ancient Celts or Gauls in Battle*, color lithograph by Vittorio Raineri, circa 1800 to 1818. From the Stapleton Collection.

Page 25: Detail of a thirteenth-century Byzantine mosaic in the Church of San Marco, Venice, Italy.

Page 26: Detail from the Bayeux Tapestry, circa eleventh century. Housed in the Musée de la Tapisserie in Bayeux, France.

Page 27 (top): The Domesday Book (1085–1086), housed in the Public Records Office in London.

Page 27 (bottom): Third version of the Magna Carta (circa 1225), housed in the Department of the Environment, London.

Page 28: Portrait of Henry VIII, painted by Hans Holbein the Younger, circa 1530s. Housed in Belvoir Castle, Leicestershire, England.

Page 29: Portrait of Anne of Cleves, fourth wife of King Henry VIII, painted by Hans Holbein the Younger in 1539. Housed in the Louvre Museum in Paris.

Page 30: Late sixteenth-century miniature portrait of Queen Elizabeth I by Nicholas Hilliard (1547–1619) Housed in the Victoria & Albert Museum in London.

Page 32: Nineteenth-century stained-glass window by the German School. Housed in the Stationer's Hall, London.

Page 34: Illuminated page from the Gospel of Saint Mark from the Lindisfarne Gospels. Late seventh century. Housed in the British Library in London.

Page 36: Historical text of the life of King Alfred, circa 1321. From the permanent collection of the British Library, London.

Page 37: Sixteenth-century engraving of John Wycliffe (circa 1330–1384) by the English School. From a private collection.

Page 38: Title page from Robert Barker's 1611 printing of the King James New Testament. Housed in the Pierpont Morgan Library, New York.

Page 39: Volume I title page of the first English dictionary, 1755, by Dr. Samuel Johnson. From a private collection.

Page 42: Detail of a bronze statue of King Arthur, 1513. Housed at the Hofkirche Museum in Innsbruck, Austria.

Page 43: Vellum manuscript page depicting King Arthur and the knights of the Round Table. Published by Antoine Verard in Paris, 1490. Housed at the Biblioteca Nazionale in Turin, Italy.

Page 44: *Tintagel*, by Arthur Ackland Hunt, 1887. Watercolor painted with gouache on paper. Housed at the Maas Gallery, London.

Page 45: Color lithograph, circa 1910 to 1920 by Howard Davie, depicting the fight between Robin Hood and Little John. Published by Raphael Tuck in *Robin Hood and His Life in the Merry Greenwood*.

Page 47: Illustration by Frank Adams depicting Dick Whittington on his way to London, from *My Nursery Storybook*, circa early twentieth century.

Page 48: 1830 oil-on-panel painting of Friar Tuck by Henry Liverseege. Housed in the Harris Museum and Art Gallery in Lancashire, England.

Page 49: *St. George and the Dragon* by Italian painter Paolo Uccello, 1470. Housed at the National Gallery in London.

Page 50: Colored drawing of Gogmagog, circa nineteenth century, by the English School. Housed in the Guildhall Library, London.

Page 51: "Diverse Manifestations of the Devil," 1881 illustration from *Sadducismus Triumphatus, Part II* by Joseph Glanvill.

Page 56: "The History of Nations," nineteenth-century plate by the Italian School, depicting Stonehenge.

Page 60: The ruins of Lindisfarne Priory monastery, Holy Island, England.

Page 61: A small Saxon church in Norfolk, England.

Page 62: Yorkminster Cathedral, York, England. The cathedral was completed in 1472.

Page 63: 1549 frontispiece of the Book of Common Prayer, written by Archbishop Cranmer.

Page 64: A view of the nave of Salisbury Cathedral, Salisbury, England. Salisbury Cathedral was built between 1220 and 1258.

Page 66: Canterbury Cathedral, built in many stages from the twelfth century to 1950.

Page 71: *Caernarfon Castle*, by J. M. W. Turner (1832–1833). Housed in the British Library, London.

Page 72 (top): *Miss Lloyd*, by Thomas Gainsborough, 1750. Housed at the Kimbell Art Museum, Fort Worth, Texas.

Page 72 (bottom): *Cottage in a Cornfield* by John Constable, 1833. Part of a private collection.

Page 73: *Head VI*, oil-on-canvas painting by Francis Bacon, 1949. Housed at the Hayward Gallery, London.

Page 74: *Reclining Figure*, bronze sculpture by Henry Moore. Located outside the Belvedere in Florence, Italy.

Page 80 (top): Opening page from the epic poem *Beowulf*, circa fifteenth century. Housed at the British Library, London.

Page 80 (bottom): Detail from a fourteenth-century page from "The Knight's Tale" from Geoffrey Chaucer's *The Canterbury Tales*.

Page 81: Title page from William Shakespeare's *Comedies, Histories, and Tragedies*, engraved by Martin Droeshout, 1623. Housed in the British Library, London.

Page 82 (top): Shakespeare's birthplace, Stratford-upon-Avon, England.

Page 82 (bottom): Fifteenth-century illustration depicting John Milton.

Page 83: Movie still from James Young's 1916 film *Oliver Twist*, which starred Marie Doro, Tully Marshall, Hobart Borsworth, and Raymond Hatton.

Page 88: Oil-on-canvas painting by Edith Mary Garner (1881–1955) depicting Romford Market. Housed at the Learnington Spa Museum and Art Gallery, Warwickshire, England.

Page 89: Lithograph by Joseph Nash depicting a banquet in the baronial hall of Penshurst Palace. Published in *Architecture in the Middle Ages*, 1838.

INDEX

A

Alfred the Great, 26
Anglo-Saxons, 25–26, 31, 34, 35, 36, 43, 44, 49, 61, 62, 73, 74, 79, 87
animals, 19, 20–21
architecture, 71, 74–7
Areas of Outstanding Natural Beauty, 11, 15, 97
art, 71–74
Arthur, King, 43–45

B

Bath, 25, 55, 71
Birmingham, 15, 17–19
British Empire, 23, 30–31, 33, 39
Buckingham Palace, 75

C

Cambridge, University of, 14, 106, 107
Canterbury, 55, 63, 65–67, 75, 81
Catholic Church, 28–29, 30, 31, 62, 63, 65, 67, 68–69, 84, 89
Celts, 24, 25, 33–34, 39, 43, 62, 73, 87
Chaucer, Geoffrey, 79, 80–81
Christianity, 25, 28–29, 34–35, 48-50, 59, 61–69, 71, 87, 96
Church of England, 29, 30, 62–63, 65-67, 68
Cornwall, 13, 39, 41, 43, 44, 56, 68, 74, 98

D

daily life/customs/pastimes, 95–98

E

education, 105–108
Edward III, King, 46, 49
Elizabeth I, Queen/ Elizabethan age, 30, 33, 59, 63, 81, 89
employment, 108–111
England
    areas/counties, 13–19
    climate, 12
    geography, 11–19
    population, 23
    size of, 23
    today, 8-9, 31, 96
English Channel, 11, 14, 27, 30
English language, 33, 35–38, 39, 40, 64
    Middle English, 35, 36, 37, 80
    Modern English, 35, 37, 38, 79, 81
    Old English, 35–36, 37, 62, 80
European Union, 9, 19, 105, 111

F

farming, 13, 14, 19, 24, 56, 87, 108
festivals, 53–59, 85
feudalism, 27, 29
finance, 17, 110, 111

food, 87–93, 97, 109
France/French, 11, 14, 27, 36, 37, 38, 44, 93

G

George, Saint, 48–49
Gloucestershire, 13, 55, 57

H

Henry VIII, King, 28–29, 30, 62, 63, 68, 75

I

immigrants, 9, 23, 31, 39, 55, 69, 96
Industrial Revolution, 15–16, 17, 31, 82, 90, 108
industry, 11, 14–16, 17–19, 109–111
Ireland, 8, 34, 44
Iron Age, 24, 74

L

language, 33–41
literature, 55, 79–84
London, 13–14, 17, 25, 31, 34, 38, 40, 41, 46, 54, 55, 58, 71, 73, 75, 76–77, 81, 85, 96, 100, 111

M

Magna Carta, 28
media, 101–102
Midlands, 14–15
music, 19, 53–54, 55, 58, 79, 84–85
myths/legends, 43–51

N

National Health Service, 102–103
Normans, 26–27, 62, 74, 75, 93, 108
Northern Ireland, 7, 101

O

Oxford, 13, 54, 59, 75
Oxford, University of, 13, 14, 106, 107, 108

P

Parliament, 28, 29, 38, 57, 62, 68
plants, 19, 20

R

religion, 61–69, 96

Robin Hood, 43, 45–46
Romans, 16, 17, 25, 34, 35, 44, 49, 62, 63, 87, 111
Royal Navy, 29, 30

S

Scotland, 7, 11, 16, 34
Shakespeare, William, 38, 79, 81–82, 84, 85
sports, 58, 98-101
Stonehenge, 24, 55, 74

T

Thames, river, 14, 17, 34, 40, 58
theater and dance, 79, 85
tourism, 14, 110

V

Victoria, Queen, 30, 68, 76
Vikings, 25, 26, 34, 36, 50, 62

W

Wales, 7, 11, 14, 29, 34, 68, 69, 96, 101, 107
Westminster Abbey, 75, 84
Whittington, Dick, 46–48
William the Conqueror, 8, 26, 27, 31, 37
World War II, 14, 23, 61, 90, 93, 109, 110

Y

York, 25, 65, 67

About the Author

Graham Faiella writes mainly nonfiction books and articles on subjects related to the sea and different countries. He is originally from Bermuda and has lived in England since graduating from Edinburgh University in 1978.

Designer: Geri Fletcher; **Cover Designer:** Tahara Anderson; **Editor:** Mark Beyer; **Photo Researcher:** Fernanda Rocha